NEW END THEATRE & BRIAN DANIELS
IN ASSOCIATION WITH SAW PRODUCTIONS
PRESENT THE EUROPEAN PREMIÈRE OF

SIT &
SHIVER

A NEW COMEDY
WRITTEN & DIRECTED
BY STEVEN BERKOFF

CAST in order of appearance

Lionel LINAL HAFT
Debby SUE KELVIN
Morris SAUL REICHLIN
Sam BARRY DAVIS
Betty BERNICE STEGERS
Mike IDDO GOLDBERG
Sylv LEILA CRERAR
Shirly CATHERINE BAILEY
Mrs Green LOUISE JAMESON

The action takes place in the East End of London

Playwright / Director STEVEN BERKOFF
Assistant Director SUSIE MCKENNA
Set Design by LOTTE COLLETT
Lighting by MIKE ROBERTSON
Stage Manager MARK STUART VINCE
Casting Agent SUE JONES 020 8308 5153
Press Agent SUE HYMAN ASSOCIATES LTD 020 7379 8420
Photography SHEILA BURNETT
Illustration PETER SIMPSON COOK
Graphic Design ANDREW CONNOLLY

Acknowledgements
Belsize Square Synagogue, Stanmore & Canons Park Synagogue,
Hackney Empire for the rehearsal space, the National Youth
Theatre, and Yarden GB Ltd for catering.

SIT AND SHIVER was first presented at the Odyssey Theatre,
Los Angeles, on 27 March 2004, directed by Steven Berkoff.

The New End Theatre's licence to present Steven Berkoff's play
SIT & SHIVER is granted by arrangement with Rosica Colin
Limited, London.

BIOGRAPHIES

CATHERINE BAILEY (Shirly)

Catherine was born in London and attended Italia Conti. She started acting aged 11 in the BBC series UNCLE JACK. At the age of 15 she played Ilse in Ted Hughes' RSC adaptation of SPRING AWAKENING directed by Tim Supple, followed by a regular role in THE WILD HOUSE on BBC1. Then followed 'TIS PITY SHE'S A WHORE at the Young Vic, starring Jude Law and directed by David Lan. More recently she appeared in THE LIFE & TIMES OF YOUNG BOB SCALLION alongside Adrian Edmondson and Nicholas Kent's WALK HARD – TALK LOUD at the Tricycle. Television appearances include HOLBY CITY, PEAK PRACTICE, RESIDENTS, MY FAMILY, URBAN GOTHIC, HIGH STAKES, THE INFINITE WORLDS OF H G WELLS, 55 DEGREES NORTH, ROSEMARY & THYME, THE MARCHIONESS, THE ENGLISH HAREM, EGYPT and THE BILL.

LEILA CRERAR (Sylv)

Leila was a member of the Mid Powys Youth Theatre before training at the Welsh College Of Music & Drama. Theatre productions include: Citizen in THE VISIT (winning the Lloyds Bank Theatre Challenge) and Lupa Marine in FRIDA AND DIEGO at the Royal National Theatre for Mid Powys Youth Theatre, Susan in MENTAL at the Edinburgh Festival, Manya in BLOOD MOON at the White Bear, Kennington, Alice in CLOSER, at the Dukes Playhouse, Eva in THE METHOD, Lisa in STONE and Kay in WALLS all at BAC, Phaedra in HIPPOLYTUS for Actors of Dionysus, and most recently the role of Cressida in TROILUS AND CRESSIDA at Theatr Clwyd directed by Terry Hands, and Emma in JANE AUSTEN'S EMMA, at the Haymarket Theatre. Television includes: Amanda in BELONGING for BBC Wales (3 series). Film includes: Mags in RAGING ANGELS (MPYT). Gwen in TWO WAY JOURNEY (Solo Spot Productions) and Amanda in TALES FROM CONEY ISLAND (Blast Films).

BARRY DAVIS (Sam)

Barry has been involved as an adviser and actor in a number of radio and television programmes and films, including SCHINDLER'S LIST, THE MAN WHO CRIED, directed by Sally Potter, THE MERCHANT OF VENICE and the forthcoming SIXTY SIX. He has appeared on the Yiddish stage, including a recent productions at the Bloomsbury Theatre and as a performer of Yiddish stories and songs. He has written a number of articles on Jewish history and Yiddish language and literature and is a lecturer at the London Jewish Cultural Centre. He teachers Yiddish at the Spiro Ark and has taught in Oxford and at SOAS.

IDDO GOLDBERG (Mike)

Iddo made his professional theatre debut last year in Shan Khan's new play PRAYER ROOM. Directed by Angus Jackson and premiered at the International Edinburgh Festival. Other credits include; Film: I COULD NEVER BE YOUR WOMAN, LITTLE TRIP TO HEAVEN, SUZIE GOLD, POT LUCK and UPRISING. Television: THE LAST RIGHTS, NATHAN BARLEY, LITTLE BRITAIN and ATTACHMENTS. Radio: FOUR STEPS TO HEAVEN.

LINAL HAFT (Lionel)

Linal has spent the past eight years living and working in Australia. Appearances there include; Film: MOULIN ROUGE, THE MAN WHO SUED GOD, SOFT FRUIT. Theatre: HUMBLE BOY, ARTURO UI, (Melbourne Theatre Company), GREAT EXPEC-TATIONS (Sydney Opera House), KISS ME KATE! (Brisbane Lyric), THE COSMONAUT'S LAST MESSAGE (Belvoir St, Sydney), SOUTH PACIFIC (Theatre Royal Sydney). Television: MARY BRYANT, FARSCAPE, THE POTATO FACTORY. Linal, together with his wife, Buster Skeggs and son, Sam, formed Shaft Productions producing and appearing in three highly acclaimed productions of plays by Harold Pinter: THE HOMECOMING, THE BIRTHDAY PARTY and THE HOTHOUSE, (which Linal also directed), as well as a musical DOT BY DOT WITH SONDHEIM and the Broadway comedy THE CEMETERY CLUB. Linal's UK appearances include: HENRY V, CORIOLANUS, PENTECOST (RSC), AFTER THE FALL, THE CHANGELING

(The National), THE OLD NEIGHBOURHOOD, EDMOND (Royal Court), LAUGHTER ON THE 23RD FLOOR (Queens), OKLAHOMA! (Palace), SCHOOL FOR WIVES (Almeida), OLIVER! (Albery). Television and film: VANITY FAIR, MINDER, THE BILL, SHINE ON HARVEY MOON, COMEDIANS. ESCAPE FROM SOBIBOR, BIRTH OF THE BEATLES, and MINDER ON THE ORIENT EXPRESS.

LOUISE JAMESON (Mrs Green)

Louise is probably best known as Rosa di Marco in EASTENDERS. She has done six other series for the BBC including TOM BROWN'S SCHOOL DAYS, DR WHO, OMEGA FACTOR, BERGERAC, RIDES, and her personal favourite TENKO, not to mention guest appearances in CASUALTY, WYCLIFFE, THE BILL and most recently DOCTORS, CIDER WITH ROSIE and THE GAME. Series for other companies include THE SECRET DIARY OF ADRIAN MOLE (YTV) and MOLLIE (Sky). Her first love however is the theatre and very shortly after finishing RADA, where she won the Shakespeare Award for Best Classical Performance, she joined the RSC for three years and played Stratford, London and America in numerous plays including ROMEO AND JULIET, RICHARD II, LOVE'S LABOURS LOST and THE TAMING OF THE SHREW. Non-Shakespearean roles included Molly in THE MARQUIS OF KEITH (with Sir Ian McKellan), Sylvia Plath in THE THREE WOMEN, Kate in PASSION PLAY (best New Play) and Nadia Polikarpovna in Gorky's BARBARIANS. She has also worked with the Royal National Theatre in DEATH OF A SALESMAN. Other theatre includes Rosalind in AS YOU LIKE IT (Regent's Park Open Air Theatre), Helena in A MIDSUMMER NIGHT'S DREAM (Old Vic), Miriam Gotchalk in MEPHISTO and Beatrice in MUCH ADO ABOUT NOTHING (both for Oxford Theatre Company), Roxanne in STICKY FINGERS (King's Head), Moll in MOLL FLANDERS (West Yorkshire Playhouse) and Mollie in SLEEPING NIGHTIE (Royal Court Upstairs). She recently filmed a short called AFTER ALICE (BAFTA nominated). Other films include MY FRIEND WALTER and STICK WITH ME KID. She owns TLC Productions Ltd, a company whose view is to explore and encourage new writing and to take a sideways look at the classics, to which end she has produced, written and directed WOTCHA WILL and premiered a two-hander, SEXWARS. Soon she will be appearing in CONFUSIONS at Windsor and a tour of ARSENIC AND OLD LACE. Early next year her own one woman show, HOTFLUSH by Helen Goldwyn, will be ready for production.

SUE KELVIN (Debby)

Most recently starred in SOPHIE TUCKER'S ONE NIGHT STAND (New End Theatre, then transfer to the King's Head Theatre). West End: Mama Morton in CHICAGO (Adelphi), Widow Corney in OLIVER (Palladium), Mme Thenardier in LES MISERABLES (Palace), Emma Goldman in ASSASSINS (Donmar Warehouse). Other theatre work includes: STREETCAR NAMED DESIRE (Royal National Theatre), RAGS (Bridewell Theatre), WILD, WILD WOMEN (Orange Tree, Richmond), TEECHERS (Northampton), GREAT AMERICAN BACKSTAGE MUSICAL (Basingstoke), ANNIE (Aberwystwyth), tours with Proteus, Resisters, SNAP, and Flying Pig Theatre Co, and UK tour of HELLO DOLLY! Television and film includes: WORST WEEK OF MY LIFE, MIKE BASSETT, KEEN EDDIE, COUPLING II, RED DWARF, BRAZEN HUSSIES, LOVE HURTS (Series II), LONDON BRIDGE, CASUALTY, RED EAGLE, SONG OF SONGS. Cabaret: GIRLS WHO WEAR GLASSES (King's Head), Pizza On The Park, The Vortex.

SAUL REICHLIN (Morris)

Saul returns to the New End stage for the first time since the sell-out British Premiere of his show SHOLOM ALEICHEM – NOW YOU'RE TALKING! which, with Singer's GIMPEL THE FOOL, has since toured 30 cities in 7 countries, including Off-Broadway and Chicago. Leading theatre roles include Valentine in LOVE FOR LOVE (National Theatre) Josef Mashkan in OLD WICKED SONGS (nominated Best Actor in 2001) Willy Loman in DEATH OF A SALESMAN. Screen roles include POINT MEN for Bond director, John Glen; Bram Fischer in MANDELA with Danny Glover; leading and key roles in THE PRISONER FILE, MISS MARPLE, POIROT, THIS LIFE.

BERNICE STEGERS (Betty)

Bernice Stegers' first fringe appearance was in Heathcote Williams' THE IMMORTALIST, a one woman show which transferred to the Young Vic, also BLOOD RELATIONS at the Young Vic. Most recent theatre includes TRIPS CINCH and THE ORCHESTRA (Southwark Playhouse), VENEZIA and MURDER AT THE GATE and THE IDIOT (Riverside Studios). Television includes TO PLAY A KING, LITTLE LORD FAUNTLEROY and TIPPING THE VELVET. Among her many film credits are Fellini's CITY OF WOMEN, Alain Tanners LIGHT YEARS AWAY and James Ivory's QUARTET. Most recently Bernice has appeared in THE PRIVATE ROOM also at the New End.

STEVEN BERKOFF (Playwright/Director)

Steven Berkoff was born in Stepney, London. After studying drama and mime in London and Paris, he entered a series of repertory companies and in 1968 formed the London Theatre Group. Their first professional production was IN THE PENAL COLONY, adapted from Kafka's story. East, Steven's first original stage play, was presented at the Edinburgh Festival in 1975. Other original plays include MESSIAH: SCENES FROM A CRUCIFIXION, THE SECRET LOVE LIFE OF OPHELIA, WEST, DECADENCE, GREEK, HARRY'S CHRISTMAS, LUNCH, ACAPULCO, SINK THE BELGRANO!, MASSAGE, STURM UND DRANG and BRIGHTON BEACH SCUMBAGS.

Among the many adaptations Berkoff has created for the stage, directed and toured are THE TRIAL and METAMORPHOSIS (Kafka), AGAMEMNON (after Aeschylus), and THE FALL OF THE HOUSE OF USHER (from Poe). His plays and adaptations have been performed in many countries and in many languages. He has also directed and toured productions of Shakespeare's CORIOLANUS (also playing the title role), RICHARD II (for the New York Shakespeare Festival), HAMLET and MACBETH as well as Oscar Wilde's SALOMÉ. He directed and performed in MASSAGE in Edinburgh and Los Angeles, RICHARD II at the Ludlow Festival, and has performed ONE MAN and SHAKESPEARE'S VILLAINS at venues all over the world. He has directed his plays and adaptations in many countries including Japan, Germany, Israel, Australia and America.

Films: Steven has appeared in include A CLOCKWORK ORANGE, BARRY LYNDON, THE PASSENGER, MCVICAR, OUTLANDS, OCTOPUSSY, BEVERLEY HILLS COP, RAMBO, REVOLUTION, UNDER THE CHERRY MOON, ABSOLUTE BEGINNERS, THE KRAYS, FAIR GAME, ANOTHER 9 WEEKS, LEGIONNAIRE, THE FLYING SCOTSMAN and PU–239. He directed and co–starred with Joan Collins in the film version of DECADENCE.

Television productions include: WEST (Limehouse/Channel 4), METAMORPHOSIS (BBC), HARRY'S CHRISTMAS (Limehouse), SILENT NIGHT (Initial/Channel 4), and Edgar Allan Poe's THE TELL–TALE HEART (Hawkshead/Channel 4). Television credits include WAR AND REMEMBRANCE, MICHELANGELO – A SEASON OF GIANTS, SINS, ATTILA, NEW TRICKS and HOTEL BABYLON.

He has published a variety of books, such as the short story collections GRAFT: TALES OF AN ACTOR (Oberon Books) and GROSS INTRUSION (Quartet Books), the production journals I AM HAMLET, MEDITATIONS ON METAMORPHOSIS (Faber and Faber), CORIOLANUS IN DEUTSCHLAND (Amber Lane Press), and A PRISONER IN RIO (Hutchinson), his autobiography FREE ASSOCIATION (Faber), a photo-graphic history THE THEATRE OF STEVEN BERKOFF (Methuen), and travel writing, essay and poetry collections SHOPPING IN THE SANTA MONICA MALL (Robson Books), AMERICA (Hutchinson), and OVERVIEW (Faber). Faber has published Berkoff's collected plays in three volumes, as well as THE SECRET LOVE LIFE OF OPHELIA. REQUIEM FOR GROUND ZERO (Amber Lane Press), Steven's tribute to September 11th in verse, is Steven's latest publication, and coincided with a run at the Edinburgh Festival, followed by a one–year anniversary performance in London.

Steven Berkoff has done a variety of voiceover work and books on tape, including Kafka's METAMORPHOSIS and THE TRIAL for Penguin Audiobooks and Henry Miller's NEXUS for Prelude Audio Books. Radio productions include the title role in MACBETH (Radio 4, available through Penguin Audiobooks) and his live music debut as the MC in CABARET (Radio 2). He recorded AN ACTOR'S TALE, a selection of his short stories, for Radio 4. CD recordings of celebrated productions of CORIOLANUS, SALOME, EAST, and THE TRIAL are available on CD visit www.stevenberkoff.com

LOTTE COLLETT (Set Designer)
Work for theatre includes MERCHANT OF VENICE (Linbury Studio, ROH for the National Youth Theatre and BBC), MURDER IN THE CATHEDRAL at Southwark and Westminster Cathedrals, THREEPENNY OPERA, THE LIFE AND ADVENTURES OF NICHOLAS NICKLEBY, THEY SHOOT HORSES DON'T THEY?, CANDIDA, OEPDIPUS THE KING, ROMEO AND JULIET, LORCA'S EARTH TRILOGY at the Riverside, OTHELLO, BLOOD WEDDING for Teatro Principal Valencia, TRIAL BY JURY in Bow Street Magistrates Court and The Creation Project, THE FEMALE WITS and OH WHAT A LOVELY

WAR, both for Covent Garden Opera Festival. Design for television includes LENIN, THE QUEST, MARVIN THE METAL EATING BABY and SPY IN THE CAB. Design for dance includes PASSPORT TO BALLET for ENB and MIND GAMES 1, 2 AND 4. Lotte has designed for Susie McKenna on A CHRISTMAS CAROL, SLAPPERS AND SLAPHEADS, ALADDIN and JACK AND THE BEANSTALK.

SUSIE MCKENNA (Assistant Director)
Susie has most recently directed SOPHIE TUCKER'S ONE NIGHT STAND by Chris Burgess (New End Theatre and King's Head Theatre). Susie is associate director at Hackney Empire and has written and directed six pantomimes for the venue including the critically acclaimed ALADDIN and JACK AND THE BEANSTALK. Last year she co-produced and directed a season of cabaret and new writing at the new Acorn Studio there. Her other productions at the Empire include her adaptation of A CHRISTMAS CAROL, FUN SONG FACTORY, SASS SOUL SEQUINS, THE ULTIMATE KNEES UP and THE BEST OF THE EMPIRE – the theatre's re-opening gala. At Greenwich Theatre she has directed THE HAPPY PRINCE and I MARRIED WYATT EARP for Musical Futures and FARM for Musical Voices. In Liverpool she directed SLAPPERS AND SLAPHEADS at the Empire Theatre and BRICK UP THE MERSEY TUNNEL for the Liverpool Comedy Festival. Productions for the Haringay Shed Theatre Company include writing and directing A GLITCH IN TIME, WHEN YOU BELIEVE, FAIRYTALE MADNESS and HEROES!

MIKE ROBERTSON (Lighting Design)
Recent credits include SUNDAY IN THE PARK WITH GEORGE, Wyndhams & Menier Chocolate Factory; MIDSUMMER NIGHT'S DREAM, Royal Shakespeare Company Tour; PREACHEROSITY, Jermyn Street; DICK WHITTINGTON, Cambridge; ANYTHING FOR A QUIET LIFE and ANTONIO, Cochrane; WIDOWS, RADA; MIRANDOLINA and A LAUGHING MATTER, Cochrane; KIT & THE WIDOW and FASCINATING AIDA, Copthorne; CLASSIC ABSURDITY, Birmingham Hippodrome; The Harare International Festival of The Arts (21 shows); BRYAN ADAMS, Royal Opera House; DAYS OF THE COMMUNE, RADA; THE SNOW QUEEN, Barbican & Cadogan Hall; THE PALACE OF FEAR, Leicester Haymarket; EXCLUSIVE YARNS, Wimbledon; SNOOPY THE MUSICAL, New Players, THE POCKET DREAM, York; THE GLEE CLUB, Octagon; SPRING PROMS, Royal Albert Hall, 28 TAKES ON LIFE (Film); THE RINK and LARKIN WITH WOMEN, Coventry; SWEENEY TODD, THE MAGIC FLUTE, THE

FLYING DUTCHMAN, A PLACE AT THE TABLE, THE TESTAMENT OF YOUTH, VITA & VIRGINIA and HYSTERIA, UK Tours. Mike has also lit many parties for clients including Elton John, Tommy Hillfiger and Dell. He has designed the interior lighting for commercial aircrafts for clients including Virgin, BA and Airbus and has lit many buildings, trade shows, conferences and events. More at www.lightingplan.co.uk

BRIAN DANIELS (Producer)
Brian has been Chief Executive/Artistic Director of the New End Theatre, Hampstead for 10 years. He is also Chief Executive of the Shaw Theatre, Euston and an Associate Producer of the King's Head Theatre, Islington. He has produced more than 100 shows over the last 10 years including SHE KNOWS YOU KNOW! (national tour/Vaudeville Theatre), LADY DAY AT EMERSON'S BAR & GRILL (national tour/West End transfer), THE DISPUTATION (New End Theatre, Theatre J, Washington DC and Jerusalem), AND ALL THE CHILDREN CRIED (New End Theatre/BAC), His recent production of SOPHIE TUCKER'S ONE NIGHT STAND transferred to the King's Head Theatre and will be at the Edinburgh Festival 2006 with a national tour to follow.

NEW END THEATRE (Producers)
New End Theatre presents the best in new and and issue–led writing, this includes musicals, comedy and classic revivals. Recent successes include: A DANGEROUS WOMAN with Fenella Fielding, BRIEF CANDLE with Denis Quilley, WEILL & LENYA directed by Ken Russell, THE DISPUTATION, BENCHMARK with Jerry Hall directed by Michael Rudman, LAST SONG OF THE NIGHTINGALE with Tracie Bennet, AND ALL THE CHILDREN CRIED with Sharon Maughan, TAKE A CHANCE ON ME with an all–star cast including Helen Lederer and Joe McGann, ALICE VIRGINIA with Susannah York, and NIGHTINGALE written and directed by Lynn Redgrave. Recent West End transfers include THE DEAD MONKEY with David Soul, PERSONALS, LITTLE WOMEN, LIES HAVE BEEN TOLD, DANNY'S WAKE and LADY DAY AT EMERSON'S BAR & GRILL. Visit the New End Theatre website at www.newendtheatre.co.uk or contact us via email to briandaniels@newendtheatre.co.uk

FOR THE NEW END THEATRE

The New End Theatre is registered in England as a Company
Limited by Guarantee No 3296703 and as a Charity No 1062498.
Registered office 27 New End, London NW3 1JD.

ACKNOWLEDGMENTS
The New End Theatre gratefully acknowledges the support of
The Kessler Foundation which is funded by The Jewish Chronicle,
The Mackintosh Foundation, The Royal Victoria Hall Foundation,
Douglas Heath Eves Charitable Trust, John S Cohen Foundation.
Lighting equipment sponsored by CAP Production Solutions
(020 8544 8668).

A NOTE FROM STEVEN BERKOFF

When Jews who are remotely religious mourn the dead, they sit for seven days in a room usually cleared of comfortable furniture and replaced with hard chairs, or even wooden boxes. This is so that they sacrifice their comfort and possessions and can cast their hearts and minds on the deceased. Friends and relations drop in to give condolences, and the deceased is honoured and their best qualities revered. Coffee, tea and snacks are imbibed as the conversation meanders its way around the dead person and then on to other things. As a child I always heard the ceremony as 'sit and shiver', which made perfect sense to me, since it seemed an expressively Jewish way of saying we are in grief and shivering our real feelings.

Only later did I learn that the word *shiva* means the seven days of mourning. It occurred to me some while ago that this setting had dramatic potential, and I tried to imagine my own family in this situation, and so the characters are drawn from some close relatives, most of whom are now dead. So this is my sit and shiver for them. Uncle Sam and Betty are very real characters in my memory. Debby is a rather stylised mother, who is always in the kitchen and seems to live there, waiting on everyone and wishing always for you to eat. Fishcakes were her speciality.

My father is deceased, a man of secrets that only death was really able to reveal. Morris is the close friend of the family, the one mensch who always manages to make good and is able to restore calm. The friend we always admired in contrast to us. Mike is the actor clothed in guilt for the deficits of the trade he has chosen, which means swathes of time out of work. He in fact envies the old-world skills.

Mrs Green is an invention but close to the Mrs Greens of memory, decent gentile ladies who did part–time jobs for the tailor in his shop. Sylv throws a sharp contrast by her reserve, and makes us aware how painfully open we can be. Lionel is just a decent human and is an amalgam of many. Uncle Sam was a famous East End character who fought the British fascists in the thirties, was self–taught and could recite Shakespeare. He was one of the greatest political speakers in the East End and gradually went blind, but he kept his incredible vigour to the end and in fact drank endless cups of tea. Although I never sat for any of their deaths, I still shiver for their memories.

Steven Berkoff, 10 April 2004

Steven Berkoff
Sit and Shiver

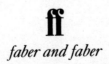

faber and faber

First published in 2006
by Faber and Faber Limited
3 Queen Square, London WC1N 3AU

Typeset by Country Setting, Kingsdown, Kent CT14 8ES
Printed in England by Intype Libra Ltd

A CIP record for this book
is available from the British Library

ISBN 978-0-571-23469-1
ISBN 0-571-23469-0

2 4 6 8 10 9 7 5 3 1

'A faultless man is possible only in a faultless world.'

Old Jewish saying

'The world is new to us every morning –
that is God's gift – and a man should believe
he is reborn each day.'

Baal Shem Tov

Characters

Lionel
Debby's husband, fifties or sixties.
Retail manager, ex-tailor, bullied by his wife.

Debby
Lionel's wife, fifties. Aggressive, warm, sentimental.

Morris
An old friend of the family, fifties.
Successful businessman.

Sam
Debby's brother, sixties.
Blind, wise, compassionate, political.

Betty
Sam's wife, sixties.
A shrew, but fond-natured. Puts up with life.

Shirly
Lionel and Debby's daughter, late twenties.
Smart, quick, wants to find a man.

Mike
Lionel and Debby's son, an actor, early thirties.
Shrewd, intelligent, poetic. A bit of a loser.

Sylv
Mike's girlfriend, late twenties.
Sweet, benign, a *shicksa*.

Mrs Green
Debby's father's former shop assistant, sixties.
Lover / mistress of the deceased.

The deceased, named Monte, was a tyrant, but
conformity means death elevates him to sainthood.
The tragedy of the departure means that all sins
are washed away by the monumental event.
We look to the good points, and try to redeem
the man so that death should have a dignity at least!
Eventually his past rolls out, via Mrs Green,
and the truth spills out with it . . .

Act One

SCENE ONE

A room is set for bereavement. There are wooden boxes in the room for people to sit on since this is a Jewish bereavement commonly known as 'sit and shivah'. I used to think of it as sitting and shivering with grief and cold, but its meaning is quite different. It generally means to sit and mourn for seven days. The custom of seven days' mourning is at least three thousand years old. Comfortable furniture is removed and replaced with hard seats to keep us alert. Mirrors are covered lest we be vain and not regard the memory of the deceased.

A husband and wife sit as they are mourning for the wife's father, a stern patriarch with a reputation for self-denial and integrity.

It is early morning in the East End of London. Music plays. Lionel and his wife Debby are arranging the 'boxes' for the guests.

Lionel So what time did you say for them to come?

Debby Come? When they want to come . . . When they feel like it!

Lionel You should have said from such an hour . . . given an indication . . .

Debby Well, who's coming at dawn? Of course they'll come, they'll turn up when they want to, when they have time . . . After work, before work, who knows? It's not a party . . . turn up at eight o'clock . . . it's a 'sit and shivah' . . .

Lionel Oh, thanks for telling me . . . I thought it was a bar mitzvah!

7

Debby So they can turn up all day, afternoon and night. They dribble in . . . as they like. They have time . . . a whole week!

Lionel A whole week . . .

Music ends.

A *broch*!

Debby A *broch*!? You curse for a week of mourning for my father . . . You say a *broch* for my father . . . May he rest in peace . . .

Lionel No! Not for your father . . . for your father I sit and shiver for a week . . . You want that? I do it . . . I do it . . . Did I complain? You want these ancient rituals, these ghetto habits from the *shtetl* . . . Habits to sit on a box . . . A week to sit on a box . . . in old clothes – *alter schmutters* – to show I feel . . . I *feel* . . . I *do* feel, yes I do, Deborah . . . Don't look . . . like she wants to kill, she looks . . .

Debby (*shaking her head*) I just . . . I just *look* at you and you begrudge . . .

Lionel *Who* begrudges?

Debby (*nervous agitation*) You begrudge for my father . . . My loving father who gave me life . . . From his loins, from him I sprang . . .

Lionel Do me a favour! And your mother . . . What's wrong with your mother?

Debby Of course for my mother – may she rest in peace – but now we're mourning for my *father* . . . Without him, there's no me.

Lionel (*turning away as if wishing there hadn't have been*) Hmm . . .

Debby I saw that look . . .

Lionel What look? . . . Whadya talking about – 'that look'? Every time I turn, you put an interpretation on it . . .

Debby You're full of resentment . . .

Lionel Okay, I'm full of resentment . . .

Debby Dad was a great man, a loving man, a *mensch* . . .

Lionel He was a *mensch*, that he was . . . I'm not denying he was a good man, although he was not a saint! I'm saying that for a week we make appearances . . . We sit on boxes . . . But I can still *feel* on a sofa . . . I won't feel any less on an armchair . . . I might even feel *more* because my *tuchis* won't be so damn stiff.

Debby What do you mean, he wasn't a saint . . .

Lionel Nothing . . . Just that he was human, like the rest of us . . .

Debby He wasn't like the rest of us . . . In those times men were different . . . They were tough because they lived through hard times . . . They didn't *kvetch* over everything . . . A divorce was unheard of . . . To my darling mother he was loyal for fifty years . . .

Lionel Hmmnn . . .

Debby What . . . 'Hmmnn'?! They loved each other!

Lionel Who's denying?

Debby When they married, they didn't have a pot to piss in . . . Forgive the expression . . .

Lionel You told me a thousand times already!

Debby But when love is strong, a man and a woman can make their bed on a sword's blade, but when love is weak, a king-sized bed is not wide enough!

9

Lionel Oy!

Debby (*pause*) Do you think there's enough food?

Lionel Plenty!

Debby I should have got more cakes . . .

Lionel But we've got the fishcakes . . .

Debby Not everybody likes fishcakes . . .

Lionel Wadya talking about . . . People *love* fishcakes, 'specially *your* fishcakes!

Debby Oh yeah, *schmoozer*! But for some it's a bit early for fishcakes.

Lionel Do you want me to run to Rinkoff's?

Debby No, not now, they'll be here soon . . .

Lionel Send Shirly . . .

Debby She's answering the door, doing the tea . . .

Lionel How many did you get?

Debby Five dozen *blintzes*, five dozen strudel . . .

Lionel Strudel?

Debby That's what most people like . . .

Lionel That's what *you* like, maybe some Danish pastries wouldn't have gone amiss . . . cheesecake . . .

Debby Cheesecake we've still got, there wasn't time . . . I just dashed in and out. Anyway, the old lady, when I went to Rinkoff's, distracted me talking about her grandson who's becoming a film director, can you believe . . .

Lionel That little kid that used to deliver bagels?!

Debby That little *shlemiel* with the snotty nose who couldn't add up . . . That *shlemiel* is now a film director.

Lionel Amazing! Well, you never know . . .

The doorbell goes.

Oops, there's the first . . .

Lionel leaves.

Debby (*to audience*) He makes me sick . . . You're a curse in my *kishkas*, you *momzer* . . . You begrudge my father's ceremony, my *tata's* 'sit and shiver', he whose shoelaces you are not fit to tie, you bastard . . . He was a good man, a good soul, and you can only sit in his shadow . . . Papa warned me . . . Why didn't I listen? He said – he had a *kopf*, he had vision that man – he said, 'Debby, the man is weak . . . He's not a bad man, but his weakness will suck the marrow out of you. He's a needer.' But my mother – God rest her soul – she worried. I was twenty-three already. Terrible thing! That's nothing. *Today* that's nothing . . . She forced me . . . She coerced me . . . 'You're twenty-three! By the time you're twenty-five, people worry – "Is there something wrong?" – and before you can blink, you're thirty . . . A *broch*! And then all you can get is *ganeff*, a pimp who thinks he is doing you a favour . . .' But *Dad* knew – my papa – what a small-minded *ganeff* he was. Such a petty, mean, tight-assed *kvetcher* . . .

Her facial expression changes as she sees Morris entering with Lionel.

Morris Debby . . .

Debby Morris . . .

Morris *Bubeleh . . . shaynalla . . .* I wish you long life and may his soul rest in heaven. I won't kiss you, I have a cold. (*He sits.*)

Debby *Gei gehsunt.*

Lionel Some tea? A cake?

Debby Sit, I'll do it . . . I heard the bell and wondered what had happened to you . . .

Morris First I had to attend to the waterworks! Ha ha, at our age it's always the waterworks!

Lionel You have to go . . . when you have to go!

Morris The prostate . . . It gets bigger and cuts off the waterworks . . .

Lionel How often do you get up in the night?

Morris It depends . . . Maybe three times . . . Sometimes two . . . It depends . . . And you? . . .

Lionel I . . . er . . . sometimes . . .

Debby (*from behind table*) Once he got up six times! Six times my sleep was broken . . . Can you believe this?!

Lionel (*embarrassed*) Come on, Deb, do me a favour with your six times . . . Maybe two or three . . .

Debby (*relishing the moment*) *Six times!* I counted, could you believe it? Six times!

Lionel Why don't you say it a few more times . . .

Debby Do something about it, I tell him . . . You can do something about it these days, eh, Morris?

Lionel Listen . . . We buy a double king-sized bed and you won't even know I'm there!

Morris Saw palmetto, that's good . . . That increases the flow . . .

Debby Please, Morris, spare me the details . . .

The kettle is now whistling.

Milk and sugar?

Morris No darling, just milk.

Lionel That's all you take – this 'palmetto' stuff?

Morris It works wonders . . . at least for me. Otherwise you can have a small op.

Lionel I've heard of the op . . .

Morris (*slowly, with warning*) Yeah, they trim the prostate but in trimming you might lose your sex drive . . . For me I don't care, but for some men it's a serious decision . . .

Lionel No, I wouldn't want anything that would interfere with my sex drive . . .

Debby Sex drive?! Hahahaha! Tell me about it . . . *Who* are you saving it for? Have the op . . . Believe me, I won't miss the sex drive – hahaha – but I'll get some sleep . . .

Lionel Why don't you tell Morris something *really* intimate!

Debby Come on, we've known Morris for thirty years . . . Have a sense of humour!

Morris Look, Debby, I can't stay long . . .

Debby Who cares how long! I'm not timing you, Morris . . . You came . . . That's the main thing – you came . . . You made a *mitzvah* . . . Daddy would be happy . . .

Lionel He is happy . . . Maybe he can see us now . . . Who knows these things?

Debby (*starting to cry a little*) Whether he is or whether he's not . . . Whatever he's doing, God bless him . . . He's happy . . .

Lionel Listen, he's out of his misery . . . I mean, Debby, why should he suffer so much? It's best now he's not suffering . . .

Debby Please God, please God, he's happy . . .

Morris He's found his peace, Deb, and I wish you peace now . . . I wish you peace and health, Lionel . . . I wish also for the children . . . Mike and Shirly, bless 'em . . .

Debby Mike'll be here later, after work . . .

Lionel It's also a relief for Debby . . . The treks to the hospital –

Debby OY VAY!

Lionel – the waiting while he had the chemo stuff they shove inside you . . .

Debby OY VAY!

Lionel (*starting to relish it*) And then after three months of chemo, when he went white as a sheet, they discover that it had spread to the glands and then another op, up the neck . . .

Debby OY! VAY! VAY! VAY!

Lionel And then the radiation . . . *Oy vay*, I wouldn't wish it on my enemy . . .

Debby *Gevalt!* What that man went through . . .

Morris (*trying to change their illness duet*) But now it's over and your dad's probably up there having a good laugh . . . seeing his friends . . . *kibitzing* . . . playing rummy . . .

Debby He *loved* his cards!

Lionel He loved them, that's for sure, and they loved *him* . . . A fortune he lost . . . Like you can't believe . . .

Debby (*sad and sombre*) Listen, it was his weakness . . . So, was it *your* money, Lionel, eh? Did he put his hand in your pocket? So he enjoyed his last years with his cronies

and a game of blackjack or rummy . . . He was a gambler
. . . That's our vice, gambling . . . The *goyim* love to
drink . . . Some are serial adulterers and some beat their
wives . . . But Papa, my dad – God rest his soul – never
once laid hands on a hair of my *mumella*, Bella, my
lovely darling mother.

Lionel It's amazing how important a man becomes when
he dies . . .

Debby So . . . What do you mean by that?

Lionel What do I mean? I mean we appreciate them
more . . . She's so quick to jump down my throat . . .

Morris (*trying to change the subject*) He was a good
man . . .

Debby When you close the shop, you lock the door. So
you should also put padlocks on your mouth!

Lionel Look who's talking! Listen, *dollalla*, no padlocks
would stop *your* mouth . . . 'cause like a Houdini, you'd
break it! Ha! Ha!

Morris He was a good man – no question – heart of
gold . . .

Debby Maybe, okay, he loved the *spieler*, the dogs and
the horses and a weekly game of blackjack . . . That was
his life . . .

Lionel I'm saying that was his life . . . That's all, that was
his life . . .

Debby (*quickly*) But the fridge was always full!

Lionel No question . . .

Debby Am I right?

Lionel Absolutely!

Debby Mum never wanted for nothing . . . Nothing!

Lionel Don't get so critical, Deb . . . I'm just saying that he loved to gamble. Morris, let me fill your cup. That's all I'm saying . . . Don't make such a deal . . .

Debby It's in the blood . . . The old world . . . The first generation, especially as he was a Romanian . . .

Lionel They gambled, they drank, they sang like gypsies.

Debby It's not so much the gambling . . . it's the getting together . . . it's the excuse for a gossip. A bunch of jokers . . . rolling out their tongues like a red carpet. Anyway, Dad never drank . . .

Lionel A *bissle*, Debby . . . Come on, he liked a schnapps now and then . . .

The doorbell goes.

Morris Ah, they're turning up!

Lionel (*handing him a plate*) Sure you won't have a cake?

Morris I'll take a small one . . . You got a small one?

Lionel There's a small one . . .

Debby (*shouting*) Shirly, get the door. Can't you hear the bell?!

Morris No, that's a *big* one.

Debby They're all the same size!

Lionel Some are bigger than others.

Morris Some are smaller than others . . . Ha ha!

Debby Shirly, did you get the door?!

SCENE TWO

Enter Sam and Betty. Sam is blind with a good feisty spirit while his wife, Betty, is loud, with a hard-done-by attitude, but good-hearted. Shirly, the daughter of Lionel and Debby, enters with them.

Shirly I'm on the phone . . . Be back in a minute . . . It's an important call.

She nips out again. Ad-lib on entrance.

Debby My life, she *lives* on the phone . . . Betty, how lovely to see you! Sam, come and sit down . . . Over here, that's it . . . Easy does it . . .

Sam Debby, you're looking better than ever . . .

Debby Sure, especially today, you joker . . .

Betty Listen, I can't say it's a pleasure, but I wish it was a happier occasion!

Lionel We always meet at funerals or mournings!

Morris If you have weddings and bar mitzvahs, you got to have, unfortunately, funerals. Us old ones have got to make room.

Sam Listen, if the rich could hire the poor to die for them, the poor would make a very good living . . .

Betty It's no disgrace to be poor . . . which is the only good thing you can say about it!

Debby At least if you're poor it's good for the waistline.

Sam They say the heaviest weight in the world is an empty pocket . . .

Debby My life, it's true . . . (*to Morris*) More cake?

17

Sam On the other hand, Debby, the prayers of the poor are heard by God before all others.

Betty So . . . so why are they still poor if He's such a good listener?

Sam 'Cause He knows the kids of the poor are the brains of tomorrow!

Lionel I like that . . .

Sam Debby, you got some tea? I'm as dry as a bone . . .

Debby You got it.

Betty I made him three cups of tea this morning . . . I don't know where he puts it!

Morris (*going over and taking Sam's hand*) Hello, Sam, it's Morris . . . I was a friend of Monte's.

Sam Morris? Morris!

Debby Morris Fine!

Sam Morris! Morris Fine, of course. Your father used to have the small deli in Hessel Street . . . They used to pickle the cucumber for Bloom's . . .

Morris That's right! Sweet and sour or new green!

Sam So how are you, Morris? Did you bring some pickles? Ha! Ha!

Betty He's such a *kibitzer*!

Morris I wish . . . I'm sad but I'm well . . . I'm sorry about your brother . . . God rest his soul . . .

Sam Listen, he's out of his misery . . .

Morris But you go on . . . You'll outlast us all . . .

Sam Please God and thank God, and apart from my sight, I'm well . . . I count my blessings . . .

Debby Here's your tea, darling.

Betty He still walks every day . . . Sometimes five miles a day . . .

Sam I like my walk . . .

Betty Never misses a day . . .

Morris You were always a walker!

Sam When I lived in New York I walked everywhere.

Morris *Tucker* – now that's a place to walk!

Betty That's a walkers' paradise!

Sam I'd walk from Delancey Street, cross Brooklyn Bridge, end up in Brooklyn Heights and back.

Lionel That's a walk!

Debby My old man can only walk to the fridge!

Lionel And back, don't forget that! Ha, ha!

Sam And there was nothing more beautiful than walking the Brooklyn Bridge on a sunny day.

Betty He can still feel the sun even if he can't see it!

Debby Is your tea hot enough, dear?

Sam And then the great view from Brooklyn Heights . . . I can remember how it was . . .

Betty Flats there cost a fortune . . .

Debby Shirly, come off the damn phone!

Sam Then the walk back . . . What a piece of engineering, that bridge. John Roebling, a German engineer built it in 1883 . . . I can still remember the music the wind made in the cables. In a car you can't hear that . . .

Betty As his eyes weakened his sense of hearing got stronger.

Sam Believe me, and I'm not sentimental, but whenever I walk across that bridge I give thanks to the poor labourers who died building it . . .

All Hhhmm . . .

Morris A lot of people died building what we take for granted, Sam, that is very true.

Debby My life, that's true.

Sam Twenty-seven. Twenty-seven died. The men worked under the water in a giant steel box called a 'caisson' . . .

Morris A 'caisson' . . . and the riverbed became the floor . . . As they dug deeper . . . the box got lower . . . the men got the bends, but what did they know in those days . . . when the caisson was at the right depth it became the platform for the huge towers . . .

Debby He's so clever, Sam.

Sam But Roebling died before he could see his masterpiece completed.

Debby Oh, what a shame.

Lionel Now that's what I call bad luck!

Sam (*laughs*) Yes, that's an understatement of the century. His son took over, but *he* got the bends, he didn't learn and supervised the remainder construction from his bedroom window in Brooklyn. See, there he is. He became known as 'the man in the window'.

Debby 'The man in the window' . . .

Lionel Who thinks of these things . . . we take so much for granted . . . (*to Sam*) How's your tea?

Sam My God, it was one of the wonders of the world. Can you imagine seeing that in 1883 . . .

Morris *Tucker*, they were smart in those days . . .

Sam But what kept me going was at the end of the walk I was going to get a fantastic salt beef sandwich from Katz's deli on Houston!

Betty He can't resist his salt beef sandwich!

Sam After a good walk nothing on earth tastes better.

Morris That's why you keep so fit. More tea, Deb?

Sam That's right . . . You can exercise the body but you unfortunately can't exercise the eyes.

Betty It's years in the workshop cutting, machining and working all day in a dusty environment . . . Terrible! Terrible!

Sam In those days there were no health laws, no ventilation, weak unions and you worked when you could . . . And if you complained the boss would say, 'Go somewhere else!'

Debby More cake, anyone?

Sam That was the life . . . You were squeezed like a sponge –

Betty Is the salmon Scottish?

Debby What else?!

Sam – and believe me you were glad to earn ten bucks for a day's pay.

Betty And believe me, you were glad!

Morris Then why did you come back to London – was it any better here?

Sam Why? To come back for her! That's why – crazy things we do for love!

Betty Believe me, you should have stayed!

Sam Where would I find another Bessie?

Betty That's for sure!

Sam Our boy Barry went to college . . . He studied and now he's an ear, nose and throat specialist . . . over there it would have cost a fortune.

Betty Over there you pay for everything!

Morris He's a clever boy, no question . . . The next generation is always more clever than the one before.

Sam Not so much cleverer . . . They have a better education 'cause they can stay longer at school.

Morris Because we worked, we slogged, we *schlepped* . . .

Sam But that's the pattern: the first generation works its fingers to the bone and the clarion call is 'Earn! Get out and earn!'

Betty Sam had a brain but he was dragged out of school and out into sweatshops as a kid of fourteen . . . He had a brain . . . He even wrote a play.

Sam Please, Betty.

Morris Get on . . . What a *kopf* he's got on his shoulders! No wonder Barry is so clever . . .

Lionel How's the cake?

Morris You're tempting me . . . The cake was good!

Debby I told you, I told you . . . We should have got more cakes!

Lionel I'll rush out . . . It'll take me ten minutes.

Debby What, are you crazy?

Betty Tell them, Sam, about the play . . .

Sam What's to tell? I fancied myself as a playwright . . . So, I wrote a play about the Cable Street riots in the East End . . . in 1936.

Betty Another Bernard Shaw he could have been!

Debby You want a cake, Sammy?

Sam A cake, sure, I'll never turn down a cake . . . So I wrote this play about what happened when Mosley, who was then leader of the British Union of Fascists – basically Nazia –

Debby (*interrupting*) I've got cheesecake or, if you like, a strudel . . .

Sam – so Mosley and his thugs tried to march down the Jewish East End of London in 1936 . . . or was it '38?

Betty The end of '38, I think.

Sam A man can forget everything except how to eat!

Debby So take a cheesecake . . . They're delicious!

Betty He'll eat anything! You get them from Bloom's?

Debby No, I go to Rinkoff's . . .

Sam So, the peculiar thing is, Mosley completely misjudged the British worker – although he himself was a blackshirt and a filthy anti-Semite, he had the effect of rallying the Gentile dock workers to the Jewish cause . . . It was unbelievable 'cause instead of winning them over he *alienated* them –

Betty You're right! Rinkoff's still make the best cakes . . .

Debby Thank you.

Sam – which goes to show that race hatred is politically inspired and not an instinctive or biological phenomenon.

Betty The salmon is to die for.

Debby So eat!

Sam That son of a bitch marched with two thousand blackshirts! Can you imagine that . . . *Two thousand!* . . . And protected by *six thousand* coppers and even so, they could not get through!

Morris Amazing . . . You know, I still come down the East End to get bagels . . . I can't help it . . . I go down Brick Lane, and the *goyim* are lining up for bagels . . . It unites the races! The common bagel!

Lionel I even saw bagels at Victoria Station . . . My life, they were lining up, more than for the other fast food!

Debby You should have opened a bagel shop! I told you!

Lionel She's right . . . I talked about it . . . I prophesied that one day the bagel would travel, become universal, like fish and chips.

Debby I told him, I said, 'Lionel, open a bagel shop . . .'

Lionel She's right!

Debby When we came back from our vacation in Miami twenty years ago, we saw bagels as the big thing . . .

Lionel It was the big thing, it was!

Debby I said, 'Lionel, Lionel, use your *kopf* for once and open a bagel shop in Hackney . . .' A small one . . . You would have cleaned up . . . I told him, I like the fillings. And you don't have big overheads . . .

Lionel She's right . . . she told me . . .

Debby Didn't I tell you . . .! (*ad-lib*)

24

Betty There's no end to what you could have put inside. I'd have helped you . . . (*Repeats line.*)

Debby (*to Lionel*) Didn't I tell you . . .!

Lionel You did . . . yes. I should have listened.

Sam . . . I can remember the barricades like it was yesterday, piled high. They overturned a truckload of bricks . . . It was wonderful, Jews fighting Nazis together with dockworkers, Irish and Cockney dockworkers . . .

Morris Debby, that cake is delicious!

Debby Cake, shmake! We could fill the bagels with smoked salmon, cream cheese –

Lionel – chopped herring, rollmops, sweet munster, salami –

Betty (*joining in*) – whitefish, codfish –

Morris – chopped liver, *schmaltz*, salmon spread –

Debby – egg salad, liverwurst, turkey . . . Turkey and coleslaw is delicious!

Betty Pickled cucumber –

Lionel – beefsteak and mozzarella . . .

> *A younger couple come in, who are the third generation: Mike, a struggling actor, accompanied by his girlfriend, Sylvia.*
> *Music. Cast freeze as they walk through.*

Sylv Oh, this is the family?

Mike (*introducing family*) Yeah, that's a friend of the family, Morris. And my dad and mom. And that's Aunt Betty and Uncle Sam. Watch out for him, he lost his eyesight. How are you? Hello, Auntie Betty – (*Unfreeze.*) – Uncle Sam . . .

Sam You've shot up, Mike, and you're looking so well . . .

Mike This is my fiancée, Sylv.

Sam I love your fiancée, my God, she's a pretty one . . . Hey, you've got a good eye . . .

Sylvia smiles, unsure whether he sees, and not appreciating the tribe's ghetto humour.

Mike Uncle Sam, you're a rascal 'cause sometimes you really almost fool me, but I do know you like to pull our legs . . .

Sam If I could see, I'd pull your girlfriend's . . .

Morris Oy! Now, now, now!

Mike I'm sorry I'm late, everyone . . . The traffic was awful . . .

Lionel The traffic *is* awful . . . soon you won't be able to move . . .

Morris Meanwhile the city makes a fortune in parking tickets . . . so why should they care?

Mike Mom and Dad, you know Sylv . . .

Mike still feels awkward with his shiksa.

Lionel Well, your fiancée's a bit of a stranger, since we only met a couple of times.

Debby So don't make yourself a stranger. You're one of the family and you don't have to stand on ceremony . . . Just pick up the phone and say, 'I'm coming over' – you don't have to book a week in advance. Just pick up the phone and say, 'I'm on my way' . . . There's always something in the fridge . . .

Lionel Exactly! Drop by . . . There's an open door: eat, have a cup of tea . . . You don't have to wait for a wedding or a funeral . . . I don't want you to come for *my* funeral . . . Hahaha!! Anyway, we're always in.

Debby Nearly always . . . Pick up the phone . . .

Lionel Invariably we're in . . . When do we go out?!

Debby (*embarrassed, smiles*) Do you have to tell the world that we have *no* social life . . . do you?

Lionel Of course we have a social life . . . *Here!* Home is where the heart is!

Debby (*aside to audience*) Gevalt! (*to the others*) Anyway, darling, it's always nicer entertaining at home.

Lionel That's right . . . They say only from your own table can you go away full!

Sam On the other hand, in America, more people die from overeating than undernourishment!

Betty Last time he went to Miami! . . . Oy! Could not believe the size of them!

Sylv I don't wish to bother you . . .

Debby Bother us? Bother us? What! Do you think we're jetting round the firmament and off to Cannes for the weekend? . . . He's right. We entertain at home.

Lionel We sit . . . Take it easy in the evening . . .

Debby *You* sit . . . I keep the house going . . . *I'm* the one who *schleps* and shops, keeps the house in order, and makes sure he's got clean underwear!

Mike Ma!

Debby Fills the fridge, takes his prescription to the chemist, makes sure he takes his pills every day: the blood-pressure pills at night and the prostate pills in the morning . . . And *I'm* the one he wakes in the night . . .

27

Lionel (*warningly*) Debby . . .

Debby He gets up ten times at night to do waterworks – if you'll pardon the expression . . .

Mike Hey, you two, stop having such a good time! . . .

Debby Come on, it's human. It's part of the ageing process and we're *all* getting old . . . Look, Mike, Sylv doesn't mind . . .

Sam 'The worms will eat us when we're dead but the worries eat us when we're alive . . .'

Lionel That's for sure!

Morris These cheesecakes are beautiful . . . beautiful!

Debby Rinkoff's, that's all that's left . . . Rinkoff's . . . Like us . . . We're the last of the Mohicans . . .

Lionel (*with smile*) Look, you don't have to sleep with me. Who says you have to sleep with me if I disgust you so much . . .

Mike Dad, please . . .

Debby Who says disgust? It's a fact of life, our parts wear out . . . But why should I sleep in the children's room?

Lionel So *I'll* sleep in the kids' room . . . A single bed . . . I should care. Then I have to climb the stairs each time I go to the toilet – forgive the expression . . .

Sam In America they say (*with a mock Yankee accent*) 'bathroom' . . . 'Pardon me, could you tell me where the bathroom is?' Hahaha!! Ha, ha!

Lionel (*temper showing*) Climb the stairs, Mike . . . your mother makes me climb the stairs . . . Do I care? She tortures me.

Debby OY VAY!

Lionel For thirty-three years I kept her and you and Shirly and all of us . . . I bless the years – believe me, I'm not complaining, I bless every time I bent down at the cutting table, every callus on my hands, the arthritis in my fingers, the ulcers in my stomach –

Debby And the prostate . . . don't forget that!

Lionel (*ignores and continues*) – *and* the prostate . . . Because it was for *you*, for my family, and now she wants me to climb the stairs . . . Do I care? She tortures me. One day I'll climb the stairs to paradise! Believe me! . . .

   He exits. Door slams.

Debby OY VAY!

   Music.

Mike (*following*) Dad!

Sam He should worry . . . I can't even see the toilet!

Betty He never complains, Sam . . . Bless him, never complains . . .

Sam Sometimes . . . I have to feel the bowl, but I can hear when I miss the porcelain . . . So now I sit, so at least I know where it's going . . .

Betty Sam!

Mike I'm sorry, Sylv . . . So sorry.

Sylv No, don't apologise . . . it's charming! No really.

Sam Oh Mike! I forgot that your lady was here with us. That's the trouble, you can forget who's in the room with you . . . You get old and you forget everything except how to eat!

Betty Mike is right, it's not very edifying . . .

Sam Sylv will forgive me . . .

Sylv (*quietly, shyly*) Of course . . . Please don't . . .

Sam What's edifying? We're plumbing, we're radiators . . . If the cars leak oil . . . what? Do I say, 'Shhhh! Don't talk about the car . . .' The car breaks wind just like we break wind . . . It's a build-up of gas . . .

Mike I can't *believe* this . . .

Betty Thank God I never had gas . . . Never . . .

Sam My wife's a marvel . . . My life, I married an angel.

Betty Listen, an angel I'm not – I'm human too . . . It's just that I don't make gas . . . Never have . . . I don't condemn it . . . Sometimes it's vulgar. There's a *place* for it. Some people can't control their *tuchis* . . . *or* their mouths!

Debby Well said, Betty . . .

Pause.

Sam Gas is the prerogative of the working classes . . . It denotes health and liberation. The middle classes and the bourgeoisie are afraid of their bodily functions since they like to be in control. They have to be in control of the workers *and* the workers' bodies, and so they equate the natural eruptions of the body with the working classes. You see, the workers are the body, and the ruling classes are the head trying to control the body and also afraid of it . . .

Betty (*to Sylv*) He *loves* to talk . . . Don't encourage him.

Sam I once read of an upper-class chap who farted at a dinner party given by the Duke of Windsor. He was so ashamed that he committed suicide the next day!

Morris Is that right?

Sam That's a true story.

Debby Oy, I can't believe what I'm hearing!

Betty 'His tongue has no bones so it's loose!' So can we drop the subject now? . . . (*Pause.*) Mike, so how's work? You acting anywhere?

Long pause.

Mike (*deeply uncomfortable*) Yeah, I got something coming up . . .

Betty *and* **Debby** Oohh!

Lionel It's a hard life . . . Believe me, I don't envy him . . .

Sam (*saving Mike from heat*) There was a performer in France – I tell no lies – who made a living by farting on stage . . .

Debby *Oy gevalt!*

Betty Sam, enough is enough, I think . . . You've got an obsession!!

Sam I swear it's true, he was called Le Pétomane, which means 'the farting man'; and he made a fabulous living breaking wind on stage . . . He could do all different kinds of personalities . . .

Morris I didn't know there were so many kinds . . .

Sam Of course . . . Like he would do a bride or a virgin on her wedding night, or an old priest after a huge meal.

Betty Feh!

Sam He threw the biggest taboo in the face of the bourgeois classes and they queued to see him do it.

Debby Oh, Sam!

Mike I'm obviously in the wrong business . . .

31

Morris So how did he get to do it? I mean, after he'd already expelled his . . . errr . . . gas? . . . Pardon the expression . . .

Debby Morris! Morris!

Sam Apparently he could inhale air through his sphincter.

Debby Sam, please . . . Must we refer to body functions on our father's memorial day? I mean, this is a holy day . . .

Sam You're right . . . I'm sorry, Deb.

Betty More tea, anyone?

Sylv I'd love another cup.

Betty What a crazy family, eh?

Lionel That's why she doesn't come round . . . We're too crazy . . .

Sylv No, I like it . . . It's . . . frank! Colourful!

Morris Then what would he do? Forgive me, but I love cheese *blintzes*.

Sam He'd play a tune, impersonate . . .

Debby Enough already! (*Beat change.*) So, is there something in the pipeline, Mike?

Mike Yes, I'm up for a new TV series . . .

Debby My son's a marvellous actor.

Lionel He *is*, and I wish the rest of the world thought so.

Mike How can you account for the bad taste of the world, right?

Debby Good, son, good!

Mike If the deserving got justice, we'd be in Utopia . . .

Debby Right, son! Ah, what a *kopf* he's got on his shoulders . . .

Mike (*encouraged*) If I got what I deserved, how come I got you for a dad?!

Debby Oy! Oy! Oy!

Lionel Listen, if you've got a head on your shoulders, it didn't come from space, you know.

Mike Hey, Dad, I was only joking . . . What happened to your famous sense of humour?

Lionel One day I flushed it down the toilet!

Debby What is this toilet talk this morning? Can't you lift your mind a little higher than your *tuchis*?

Sam We're all thinking of Dad and we're all grieving for him, but sometimes grief brings out something . . . Like it loosens you up, grief can also liberate.

Morris Listen, Mike, your father worked hard all his life. He never stinted . . . I know how he *schlepped* from the East End to the West End every day fulfilling the orders, and they wouldn't pay him a living wage . . . They wanted you to work for nothing . . .

Debby True, true.

Lionel We *all* worked hard . . . I wasn't alone . . . *You* worked hard, we all worked, and a twelve-hour day was normal then. No unions . . .

Morris Or very weak ones . . . We were paid seventy-five cents to cut a pair of pants . . . So I went into leather . . .

Debby *Tucker*, Morris, you did well . . . he *knew*!

Morris What can I say? It was the time of leather . . .

Lionel You had a touch, a magic touch – no question . . . Some people have it . . . You have it . . . He knew in the sixties that kids wanted *leather* . . .

Morris So I went to India.

Debby Can you believe that – to *India*! What a *kopf*!

Morris First they made up dozens, then scores, then *thousands*!

Lionel Everyone got into leather . . .

Sam An empty purse is just a piece of leather!

Morris Johnny Gold made a fortune in Carnaby Street!

Mike Oh yeah?

Lionel It was the demise of the made-to-measure suit . . . a proper suit, a decent suit, where you knew your client for *years*! Like a dentist knows his patient . . . You'd sit, show them the cloth . . . Sometimes you'd drape the cloth over their shoulders, just to give an impression in the mirror . . . A good weight, it had to be a good weight, at least sixteen ounces . . .

Sam Those towers weighed seventy thousand tons.

Mike Shh! Sam, he's telling a story.

Lionel And then you'd measure and give at least two or three fittings, and each fitting saw the gradual growth of the suit. A small adjustment here, a ripple in the back to be taken out, stage by stage, like painting a portrait . . .

Debby More tea, cakes anyone? Don't let them go to waste!

Lionel They'd stare in the mirror . . . It was a birth . . . I swear, I am not exaggerating. The first time he slips it on and he feels his arm slide into the satin lining – like liquid – and then he checks the cut . . . The lapels must

34

be perfect . . . no bumps or notches . . . a smooth line . . . and then he and the suit would be one. (*Applause.*) A year or two later he'd come back, as an old friend, and then the children . . .

Morris I tell you . . . One *knew* a Hyman suit . . . When you saw it, there was a certain fall in the drape, a low swing in the lapel . . . It was full in the chest . . .

Debby (*cynical*) Yeah, but he went poor making it because you could get a ready-made for half the price . . . And so each week he'd get less and less orders and it used to break my heart to go into the shop and see him just sitting there all day sometimes . . .

Mike I still got the suit you made me for my bar mitzvah. Lucky it wasn't a cold day. It came up to here. It was like a mini-skirt. It was too short. I froze my arse off.

Lionel You're not funny, mate . . . In the end I took in alterations . . . That's right . . . Other people's, other tailors' mistakes I'd alter. And sometimes kids would bring in their stinking trousers to have the legs narrowed, and they'd never even had them cleaned . . .

Debby He's right. They had no self-respect . . .

Lionel They stank from their *farshtinkener* farts . . .

Debby Please. Lionel, not again with the . . . *tuchis* . . .

Lionel So I thought, enough's enough . . .

Sam At least you, Lionel, were an *artist* . . . I was only a trouser-cutter . . .

Betty You were too much of a dreamer.

Sam I had no patience . . . I wanted to travel, see the world, explore . . .

Betty He even wrote a play.

Mike What was the play?

Sam I told you . . . It was about how the people of the East End in London crushed the beginning of the Nazi movement in England, which, believe me, was starting to grow . . . 1936!

Debby More cake anyone?

Morris Nah, I'm stuffed.

Sam A hundred thousand gathered to stop it and they did, and never again did fascists in uniform walk through England's streets. A new law was brought in to stop them . . .

Mike Oh yeah. I remember you telling me, Uncle Sam.

Sam I told you, so don't ask . . . Forget writing, *shmiting*, I should have gone into leather, but it was a much younger generation . . .

Morris Remember I offered you . . . I said, 'Sam, come in with me . . . Leather is the future!' Didn't I say that? You can't say I didn't tell you!

Sam I couldn't stand what I read of the sweatshops in Calcutta . . . I mean, you think *we* had it bad. It was luxury compared to over there, with children used as slave labour . . . I couldn't take it. Look, I'm not blaming you, Morris, you've got to go where the *gelt* is . . . If not you then someone else . . . The dye from the huge vats gave you cancer in no time and the acid and the grease rots your fingers off . . . A life expectancy of thirty-five to make a swinging Carnaby Street jacket . . .

Debby Who wants some nice fishcakes?

Lionel Is fur any better?

Sam It's the same . . . You exploit or torture dumb helpless animals, and if you can do it to animals you can do it to human beings. You start with animals and work your way up . . .

Morris Sam, I love you but don't lecture me. I'm a manufacturer now. I only buy the skins. I know the trade is barbaric, but if we trade with only those whose standards we respected we'd be a poor third-world country . . .

Betty He's right, Sam.

Morris What cheap means is that others live in poverty, it's the law of nature. We sell arms to maniacs so that we can keep unemployment down and a few bastards rich!

Debby If you have money, people think you are nice, handsome and can sing like a bird. More tea, coffee?

Mike 'The man who thinks that anything can be accomplished with money is likely to do anything for money!'

Sam Mike, you're right! He's got a shrewd head . . .

Debby (*from behind table*) Come on, nobody's eating the cakes!

Morris 'Yet with money you can marry off even a grandmother!' (*Laughs.*)

Lionel 'Money in the pocket means peace in the house . . .'

   Cake-eating ballet.

Sylv What do you call these cakes?

Debby *Fattening!* That's what you call them . . . or you can call them *blintzes*.

Sylv *Blintzes!* What a wonderful word . . . What's in a *blintz*?

37

Sam Mom made them once with mangos!

Lionel Wait, wait, Sylv, it's a pastry with cheese and sugar and sometimes raisins, but the cheese has to be ricotta . . .

Debby It's not so much a pastry, more a pancake . . .

Lionel Okay, a pancake . . .

Debby And it's made with eggs, raisins . . . Some use coconut –

Betty – and flour. Don't forget the flour, otherwise it won't bind . . .

Debby Of course, the flour . . . How can you make it without flour?

Betty Beat three eggs with water and milk until they're frothy, then you gradually add the flour . . .

Debby But you've got to sift it with baking powder and beat the mixture until it's smooth . . .

Betty Use a small frying pan and wipe it with a paper towel dipped in vegetable oil . . .

Debby But *heat* it!

Betty Of course you heat it! What do you think?

Debby Then you've got the batter and you pour it into the pan . . .

Betty Then you fill each *blintz* with a tablespoon of whatever you like . . .

Debby Some like cheese, some like raisins, some like –

Betty – fish! I've heard of *blintzes* made with fish . . .

Debby With *fish*! Yuk, I don't believe it . . .

Betty With fish . . . I *swear*, with fish!

Debby Then you roll it up, fold the ends, and put it in a casserole . . .

Betty You dab it with margarine . . .

Debby Butter's better!

Betty Then you bake it until it's a delish golden! Hmm . . .

Lionel And that, Sylv, is a *blintz*!

Sylv Gosh, you made these yourself, Mrs Levin?

Debby No, these I bought at Bloom's 'cause I needed a lot, but usually I make them myself . . .

Sam I'm starving! You've given me a monstrous appetite for *blintzes*!

Sylv I must say, they're awfully good . . . (*feeling bolder*) Tell me, where does the expression 'sit and shiver' come from . . . I mean, why do you call it that? Mind you, I like the sound of it . . . You shiver for the lost and beloved and their warmth has gone out of you . . . So without the warmth and their love, you shiver – metaphorically of course . . . Is it something like that?

Morris (*surprised*) That's very nice.

Sam Poetic.

Debby Nah! I don't think so, but who knows these things? You do it because you saw your father do it and *his* father and mother, but a lot of people can't be bothered any more . . . But I wanted to do it for Dad because he was such a saint . . . He was a fine man and I wanted to honour his memory.

Lionel No one's touching the fishcakes!

All ad-lib: 'I made them,' 'Bust a gut here, I got blintzes coming out of my ears,' 'Full to the brim,' etc.

Sylv So what's 'sit and shiver'?

Mike It's not really shivering, it's *shivah*, the Hebrew for 'seven', and so for seven days you sit, *shivah*, mourn and sit on boxes so that you should be humble and remember the person who has passed away . . .

Morris And in real tradition you should even cover the mirrors so we shouldn't see ourselves and be self-conscious or vain . . .

Debby Now you tell, so let's cover the mirrors!

Lionel There's no need . . . It's for the orthodox, the *frummers* . . . We don't *need* to do it!

Debby Do it! Do it! Lionel, get some towels and we'll cover the mirrors . . .

Lionel Do me a favour, Debby . . .

Debby Get the towels . . . Don't look in the mirror . . .

Sam Don't do it on *my* account . . . *I* haven't looked in a mirror for ten years!

Betty *Then* he had hair.

Lionel goes to the bathroom and gets towels and starts to cover the mirrors.

SCENE THREE

Morris So, Mike, you working on anything?

Mike No, I'm waiting for something that may or may not materialise . . . But I'm on the short list . . .

Morris Ah!

Mike The director likes me but it depends on who plays the other part.

Morris Oh!

Mike 'Cause he's trying to match up looks since we're meant to be a family . . .

Morris I see!

Mike The casting woman likes me, so she's put in a good word . . .

Morris Good!

Mike But they may be looking for a name, you know . . .

Morris Oh yeah . . .

Mike So what can you do?

Debby *You're* a name . . . Haven't you got a name?! He played a lead in *EastEnders* last year . . . Ten million people saw him . . . Ten million!

Morris Amazing . . .

Mike No, I mean a *real* name . . .

Morris So what's a *real* name?

Mike Someone who pulls in the punters – marketable . . .

Morris I see . . .

Debby How can you be marketable unless you are seen! You start off unknown and then you are marketable!

Mike I know . . .

Morris It's a tough life . . . My God, it's a really tough life . . . They want you to be experienced and successful but they won't give you the *opportunity* to be experienced and successful.

Mike It's not such a tough life, Morris. In a way *your* life is tough. You know where you're going to be tomorrow and then the next day and the next . . .

Morris (*smiling at everybody*) Thank God!

Mike Exactly! I don't know where I'll be . . . I don't know when I'll be working and, when I do, then I'm in heaven for two months, three months, but it has to end, and then you savour your freedom for a few days . . . But *you* know where you'll be every day of your life . . . Forgive me Morris, but *your* life's *predictable* . . .

Debby Michael!

Morris Again, thank God . . . Unpredictability is not for me . . .

Mike (*to himself*) One day you wake up and you wonder if you're ever going to work again . . .

Morris *Oy gevalt!*

Mike But then you get a call and its like a thrill – you're alive! Your nerves are on edge! It's an *adventure*! Is *your* life an adventure, Morris? No disrespect . . .

Debby Michael!

Morris (*to group*) Adventure I can do without now, but believe me, in my early days I had plenty of adventures . . .

Debby You'll always work, Michael . . .

Sam (*supportive*) He's resting! Listen, he needs to rest. Why should a worker feel guilty about not working every day of his life? It's no longer necessary . . . But we're made to feel guilty and so we create gluts and over-production and destroy the environment just so we can go to work every day . . . He's an actor, an artist . . . It's not like being a trouser-cutter ten hours a day for forty years . . . That is a rest!

Mike Sam, I wish I was a trouser-cutter . . .

Debby He's *mishuga*.

Mike Sometimes I wish I had the magic in my fingers to transform a piece of cloth . . . to create with it . . . to change it from one element to another . . . Dad didn't want me to become a tailor so he never taught me . . .

Debby Thank God!

Lionel It was a dying trade, that's why . . .

Mike I know that's what you always said, but I would have learned something . . . How to use my hands, a skill, a piece of magic, how to use my time, my precious breath –

Lionel He's better off as an actor . . . Did you see him in *EastEnders*? Marvellous!

Debby All our relatives phoned!

Mike – knowing something fundamental, where it doesn't matter what you look like, *are* like, whether you fit in, are part of the team, appeal to some stinking *schmuck* who doesn't know his arse from his elbow . . .

Debby Miiichael!! Do you mind? It's Zayde's memorial! This is shit and shiv . . . shit and . . . (*Dramatic pause as she realises what she has just said.*) . . . Oh my God! *Sit* and shiver . . .

Sam Hahahahahahaha! Listen, that was funny . . .

Morris Hehehehehehe!

Mike Shit and shiver . . . hahahaha!

Debby So what! A slip of the tongue! So kill me for it . . . It's all that *tuchis* talk from before . . . My life, it's affected me . . .

Sylv Go on, Michael. Tell your story.

Mike (*to himself*) So each day when I'm not working, I wonder what the day is, what can it hold, what does it

43

mean, what can I do, who can I phone, who can I see, who can I write to, who can I ask, what can I make, how can I exist . . .? But the worst is that the world is full of life . . . There's so much life out there: packed, loaded with potential, with continents to explore, rivers, cities, forests, deserts, music . . . and I can't seem to touch it even though I have the *time*!

Debby (*in contrast to Mike*) Sylvia, have another *blintz*.

Sylv They're delicious . . .

Sam I'll have one more even though I have been stuffing myself . . .

Debby Betty, have a cake.

Mike . . . I have the time, but I can't move . . . I feel fruitless . . .

Morris It's a tough life for an actor.

Mike I should suffer . . . I should wait, sit, pace, smoke, watch TV . . . call the agent . . . I have been trapped by the big con: *something may turn up*! That's why I envy the trouser-cutter . . .

Sam Hahaha! He envies the trouser-cutter . . .

Sylv He's not serious. What he means is that he respects him for his skills. He admires artists and craftsmen. He has compassion for them . . .

Morris That's important . . . 'When a man has compassion for others, God has compassion for him . . .'

Sam Romanticism for the working class – the appreciation of skills evolved over five thousand years, and then destroyed in a few generations by machines . . . We are no longer needed.

Betty Sam, Sam you're shouting.

Sam Only machines matter, and entrepreneurs . . . And if it can be done by machine, so be it . . . Let it be done, thy will be done. It's better, and new skills will evolve, like Shiatsu massage and new and yet undiscovered forms of greed.

Debby I've never understood what all the fuss is about. I can't even work my VCR. WWW dot dot dot! Madness!

Sam But you, Michael, you – nothing can replace *you* . . . Who can replace you – the actor? You are vital: the storyteller, the speaker, the *interpreter*. You're vital – a man who knows how to speak can dominate the world! You bring us the fire from the gods, you bring Shakespeare to life. Can machines do that?

Betty *Oy Gott in Himmel!* He doesn't stop!

Sylv It's fascinating . . .

Sam *Words* are magic, Mike, not suit pants! *Words* move the masses! Trouser pants *cover* the arses of the masses!

Debby Sam, please, it's . . . (*taking her time to say it*) er, *sit and shiver* . . .

All clap.

SCENE FOUR

Lionel So, Sylvia, we're a strange bunch, eh?

Sylv (*awkward, straightforward*) Oh no, it's very interesting . . .

Lionel You find us a bit odd, eh? A little noisy, a bit . . . what shall I say . . . too loud? Open?

Debby She takes us as she finds us . . . Don't embarrass her . . .

45

Lionel Who's embarrassing her? . . . Do I embarrass you, Sylvia?

They all look at Sylvia.

Sylv Oh no, I'm not embarrassed.

Betty Are you a natural redhead?

Sylv Yes.

Betty Pretty.

Sylv I like the openness, like people are free . . .

Betty Free with their tongues . . . They know how to exercise their tongues, if nothing else!

Sylv But that's very charming . . . in a way . . . We never did . . . At home, we held it in . . . like we stifled it . . . never let it out . . . so it got sour . . . and sometimes it even made us ill . . . 'cause we were afraid to speak, to tell each other what we really thought. So we talked about other things, indifferent things, like things that didn't touch us . . . didn't reveal our truth . . . our inner lives . . .

Betty With some you can have too much inner life!

Sam They say it's healthier out than in . . . And that goes for the head too . . .

Sylv So we talked about things outside . . . What we saw, what films, what was on TV, where we went on vacation . . . but never what was *in* us, which I think is warmer, because it's deeper, has soul and feelings . . . what means something, really means . . . what we love and hate . . . So we become strangers after a while . . . We run out of words . . . We'd sit almost in silence . . . Frozen, numb, wondering who was going to speak next. Should I say something? What should I say? I'm just going to say . . . it's on the tip of my tongue . . . Well, someone else comes

46

out with something and it's exactly what I am going to say. It's the same words almost word for word . . . I feel sick . . . I want to scream . . . just anything! Shout, sing, swear, hug someone . . . And there I was, frozen, with a sentence ready formed in my mind, ready to be let out like on an assembly line . . . Someone saying the same sentence . . . It was unbelievable . . .

They all stare, slightly bewildered, since she has made them all conscious of what they have been doing unconsciously for generations. There is a long silence, nodding at what she has said. Eating. Silence. Frozen.

SCENE FIVE

Debby (*pause*) So Sylvia, where you going on holiday this year?

Sylv Oooh!

Mike What's the matter?

Sylv She said it . . . She said it!

Mike Said what? What did she say?

Sylv What was on the tip of my tongue . . . what the other person said . . .

Lionel So she's a mind-reader . . . Believe me, my wife's a mind-reader . . . Ha ha!

Debby So what's so funny? It's a normal question to ask – did I say something funny?

Sylv No, no, I'm sorry, Mrs Levin . . . It's what they say, what people say when they don't know what to say . . . They say *that*, *that's* what they say . . . when they're uncomfortable with you . . . *Holidays!*

47

Sam (*pause*) I'll tell you what's on *my* mind . . . This cake – it's moreish . . . Once you start you can't stop . . . Is there any more cheesecake, Debby?

Debby (*stung*) I *like* to know where people go on holidays.

Lionel Dive right in, there's loads left.

Debby is pouring tea for everyone.

Mike We're going to hike the Highlands . . .

SCENE SIX

Shirly, Mike's sister, comes in.

Shirly Hi, everyone!

Debby I don't believe it . . . She's arrived . . .

All stand and shift.

Shirly Sorry, everyone, I was on the phone . . .

Sam An hour on the phone – *oy vay*! I don't envy your bills . . .

Shirly It was important, believe me.

Morris How are you, darling? I wish you long life . . .

Shirly Thank you . . .

Betty (*kissing her*) How are you, darling? So when you getting . . . er, you know, settling down?

Shirly Settling down, Auntie Betty? When I'm dead I'll be settling down!

Debby That's how they talk today . . . Can you believe how they talk? And don't use the phone when *we* sit and shiver!

Shirly Oh, Ma, give me a break!

Debby You should *respect* your grandfather . . . God rest his soul . . . (*She begins to sob*) What he did for you, for *all* of us . . . The man was working in a sweatshop from a thirteen-year-old, *schlepping* huge parcels down the streets, studying how to be a tailor and never taking a day off . . . never!

Mike Come on, Ma!

Sam Is it true he *never* took a day off?

Lionel But he took the evenings off to go to the *spieler*!

Debby (*to Sylv*) So he had a little relaxation . . . He deserved it . . . It was his weakness . . .

Shirly There's some more tea in the pot . . . Who wants some?

Sam Just a drop, a half-cup to wash it down, Shirlila.

Sylv I wouldn't say no . . .

Mike No thanks . . .

Morris You making any coffee?

Shirly Sure, Uncle Morris, anyone else want more coffee?

Lionel (*to Morris*) I could go for a nice cup of coffee . . . She makes a lovely cup – grinds it, the lot . . .

Debby You know you're not supposed to drink coffee. You'll be up all night!

Lionel So for one day I drink coffee . . . Big deal!

Debby Interferes with the what's-it . . .

Lionel Why don't you show them my X-rays? She can't keep anything to herself, this woman . . .

Shirly I'll make you a weak cup, Dad . . .

49

Lionel Bless you, darling. With just one brown sugar . . .

Mike Okay, in that case I'll have a coffee too . . . No sugar, unless you've got honey . . .

Shirly Now we've got honey in the house!

Debby Especially for you, Michael, for when you come, 'cause I know you love honey these days . . .

Lionel Shirly, in that case, give *me* honey . . .

Sylv If everyone's having coffee, then I'll have coffee too.

Shirly You don't have to, Sylvia, 'cause there's still tea in the pot . . . It's not a problem . . .

Sylv You sure?

Shirly Sure I'm sure, but I think the pot's cooled down and there's nothing worse than lukewarm tea, so I'll make a fresh pot . . .

Sylv In that case, Shirly, coffee is fine . . .

Shirly Believe me, it's not a problem . . .

Sylv I don't want to be the only one drinking tea . . .

Sam I'm gasping for this half-cup, Shirly . . .

Shirly I'm making a fresh pot, Uncle Sam . . .

Sam I promise you, I don't want a fresh cup . . . Just pour a half-cup, be a dear . . .

Betty Give him his half-cup, Shirl, he's got some cake in his throat . . .

Debby Don't feel guilty, Sylvia . . . I'll join you for a cup of tea . . . Not too strong, Shirlila . . .

Morris I've never had honey in coffee . . .

Mike It's really nice . . .

Morris Shirly, just one spoonful of honey . . .

Sam Shirl, you're right. The tea *is* a bit lukewarm . . .

Shirly I told you . . .

Sam And it's a bit . . . er, too strong . . .

Betty She told you . . .

Sam Listen, I didn't want to make a pot just for me.

Debby It's not just for you, I'm having . . .

Shirly Meanwhile, I'll put the kettle on . . .

She goes out for a moment.

Debby My father – God rest his soul – loved a glass of tea with a slice of lemon. Oh, how he loved that . . .

Morris That was the style . . . That's how they drank it in the old days . . .

Sam I love tea with lemon . . .

Debby Then have some with lemon . . . (*shouting*) Shirlila! Shirl! Shirly!

Shirly (*offstage*) Whaaat?!!

Debby Is there any lemon in the kitchen . . . in the bowl?

Shirly (*offstage*) Can't see any!!

Debby There should be half a lemon in the fridge!

Shirly (*offstage*) Oh yeah, but it's a bit shrivelled.

Sam Doesn't matter . . .

Debby Shirl, that's OK, we only need a bit – just squeeze that! (*Pause.*) Dad loved his lemon tea, bless him . . .

Sam I love lemon tea after cheesecake, to wash it down.

Morris Believe me, you can drink too much milk . . .

Debby Dad used to say that milk wasn't good for you . . . He had such wisdom, *tucker*, knew so many things, but

51

he couldn't say no . . . If anyone came to him for a handout, Dad's hand was in his pocket!

Shirly comes back in.

Shirly That's why we were always poor . . . Or so you told me . . .

Sam 'They say the door which is not opened for a beggar will open for a doctor . . .'

Debby Sam, you're so right! He hardly had a day's illness. He was poor but happy, how many can say that?

Sam Believe me, not many! Is this my tea, Shirl?

Debby Married to my mother for fifty years and never, *never* did he betray her with a *shiksa* . . .

Mike Ma!

Debby (*noticing Sylv*) Pardon the expression.

Betty Why a *shiksa*? . . . He could always mess around with a Yiddisher girl?

Debby Listen, Yiddisher girls don't run around with married men . . . No disrespect, Sylvia! . . .

Shirly Oh Ma, grow up!

Debby Shirly, I'm not naive, I wasn't born yesterday . . . But in general, Yiddisher girls don't play around, that's all I'm saying . . .

Betty It's true! How many nice Jewish girls run off leaving kids, divorcing, marrying again, getting new kids . . . and leaving them as well? Not many!

Sam Ha! Ha! Christmas . . . The kids don't know who to spend the holidays with!

Morris *Schtipping* isn't everything in life!

Debby Morris, please don't use that language, not on a day like this . . .

Morris Debby, I'm sorry, I'm sorry . . . I mean, I'm agreeing with you . . . Family are important . . . They are the most important thing there is . . .

Debby I agree. For us, family is everything . . . That's how we are . . .

Morris For them, it's the quality of their erection!

Shirly Morris, what's going on with you? Are you drunk?!

Sam Any more of those cheese *blintzes*?

Debby Shirly, were there any more of those cheese *blintzes* in the fridge?

Morris I'm sorry if I offended anyone . . . I'm sorry.

Shirly There's some strudel left . . .

Sam Strudel I also love.

Betty Sam, you should watch your waistline.

Sam If I could see my waistline, believe me, I'd watch it!

Morris Lately I always seem to offend someone . . .

Sam In a way you're right . . . In a capitalist society, promiscuity is rife . . . You want more and if you're told, 'Don't deny yourself, get rich!' how can you restrain one part of yourself? Your values are determined by acquisition, whereas in Marxist states your values are communal . . . towards the family . . .

Shirly You mean that they don't fool around in China?

Mike Nice one, Shirl!

Sam They don't feel compelled to, and that's the difference . . . Whereas if sex is a commodity and that's how it's sold – in movies, the press, TV – why shouldn't you have the best commodity?

Betty With me he's got the best commodity!

Sam That's right! Bessie's commodity is *her*, her *being*, her life with me. If I reduced her commodity to sex – if that was as important or even more so – I would have taken off a long time ago . . .

Betty Oh, thank you very much! I would have bought you a bus ticket.

Morris Listen, if you're going to do something wrong, at least enjoy it!

Suddenly they hear the doorbell.

Debby Shirly, answer, the door, *dollalla* . . .

Lionel I wonder who that could be?

Debby Who could it be? It's a visitor . . .

Shirly leaves to answer the door. The others quietly listen.

Shirly (*offstage*) Mrs Green . . . Oh, I'm so sorry that I don't remember you, but Mother will . . . You knew my grandfather . . . So please come in . . .

Shirly and Mrs Green, who is about sixty, both enter.

Shirly Mother, this is Mrs Green . . . She was a friend of Zayde's . . .

All freeze.

Mrs Green That's his daughter. This is his family. There's Mike. Oh, dear God, help me. I hope they understand. I hope I can make them understand.

End of Act One.

54

Act Two

Continuous with Act One.

Debby A friend of dad's . . . Oh, wonderful . . . Come in, come in . . . We've just made some tea . . . I'm sorry we didn't meet before. My husband, Lionel, this is Mike and his fiancée, Shirly, my daughter, Morris, Sam, Betty . . . or did we?

Introductions all round. They all feel awkward, since she is obviously not Jewish.

Mrs Green I used to help out sometimes in the shop on Saturdays when it got busy . . .

Debby Oh yes? You were the Saturday help?

Mrs Green That's right . . . Wrap the parcels, sometimes sew on a button, lengthen the trousers . . . or shorten them, as the case may be . . .

Shirly Really? Would you like sugar in your tea?

Mrs Green Oh, that's very kind . . . Two, please . . . I won't stay long . . . (*She notices the boxes.*) Oh, are you moving shortly?

Lionel No, Mrs Green, we put wooden boxes in a room to mourn the dead. It's an old Jewish custom . . . not to comfort ourselves . . . Like wearing black, if you like . . .

Mrs Green What a beautiful custom . . .

Mike Also, we should rip our clothes, wear something with a tear . . .

Mrs Green How fascinating . . .

Mike Yes, we're full of mad customs . . .

Debby It's tradition.

Mike I remember you now . . . When I was a kid I used to go to the shop and watch Grandad . . . Sometimes I'd do errands for him . . . Twenty years ago, right?

Mrs Green Yes, that's right . . . I remember you, too . . . Mr Hyman let you play with his shears and cut some scraps . . . Thank you. It's amazing. Did you become a tailor also?

Mike No . . . actually Mrs Green . . . I, er . . . took up acting.

Mrs Green Oh, how wonderful. Are we going to see you in anything soon?

Debby (*jumps in*) Mrs Green, you want some strudel, cheesecake?

Mrs Green No, thank you.

Lionel Fishcake, *blintzes*, coffee or tea, whatever you like.

Debby I made them!

Mrs Green Thank you. I'm all right, maybe later. Well, er, I won't stay long . . . But I needed to talk to you . . . to clear the air . . .

Debby (*on alert*) The air needs clearing? That I didn't know . . .

Mrs Green You see, I was very close to Monte, your father, Mrs Levin.

Debby He was a loving man. Everybody loved him . . . He was that kind of person . . . Everybody had a good word . . .

Mrs Green . . . Yes. Oh it's so difficult . . . I . . . er, loved him too!

Debby What do you mean, you loved him?

Sam 'Love your neighbour as yourself' is the great parable of the Torah . . .

Mrs Green But I didn't love him like a neighbour . . .

Debby Noooo . . .? So how *did* you love him? Go on – don't be *shtum* suddenly – let it out!

Lionel Hey, Debby! Let her speak . . . Go on, Mrs Green.

Mrs Green It's so hard for me . . . You can't imagine how hard it is for me to come here . . . I couldn't sleep for a week!

Debby So spit it out and then you can sleep!

Mike Shh! Ma.

Mrs Green It's hard . . . it's so hard to tell . . . what happened . . . Don't . . . please don't be angry with me. Though I know you can't help it . . . and I understand . . . Oh, this is terrible . . . I was just a Saturday help in the shop . . . that's all . . . and I saw how hard he worked and how he suffered when a day might pass with hardly any customers . . . and so he spoke to me. He confided in me and slowly . . . You know how it happens . . . slowly something touches your heart. I had no one . . . I was divorced . . . so we comforted each other . . . But I didn't wish to take him away . . . I didn't wish, I swear. But love will find a way in . . . no matter how hard you fight against it . . . and believe me, believe me I did . . . I did fight against it . . . and so . . . yes . . . we did . . . became . . . we were lovers for . . . thirty years . . . and I can't live with the secret any more . . . I can't, and now Monte has passed on . . . I felt I had to tell you . . . I felt I had to honour his memory . . .

Debby Oy! And *this* is what you come here to tell me?! In my house where we are mourning my father?! (*Turns away from Mrs Green.*) I can't believe she's saying . . . (*to her husband*) Can you *believe* what she's saying?! . . . Tell me what's going on . . .

Lionel Why are you doing this? What are you trying to prove?

Mrs Green Please, I didn't wish to hurt you . . . But I needed to mourn him too . . . I needed to tell you . . .

Debby She's lying! My father *never* had nothing to do with a *shiksa* . . . Money she wants . . . The slut wants money!

Shirly Ma! Don't speak like that . . . (*to Mrs Green*) . . . You were Grandad's *lover*?

Mrs Green Yes . . . And we had a son together . . .

Debby *Ahhhhh gevalt!*

Debby faints. Music.

SCENE TWO

Everyone jumps into freeze position and starts scene.

Lionel There, there, there! She's feeling better . . . Ahh! That's better . . . *Oy vay!* What a story.

Betty There . . . Give her some tea with a shot of schnapps . . .

Shirly She's had enough schnapps . . . Just let her sleep. Let's get her to the bedroom.

Debby (*weakly*) Is she still here . . . Is she?

Shirly No, no, she's just going . . . She's *mishuga* . . . Pay no attention . . . She'd had a fantasy about Grandad thirty years ago . . .

Sam So where's the . . . er . . . son?

Betty Sam, don't make it worse.

Sam Worse, worse, that's not worse! It's a fact of life . . . Nature has no morality . . . Thank God nature is without morals or we all would have perished . . .

Morris I have never heard such *dreck* – pardon my French – in all my born days . . . A sweeter man didn't walk the earth . . . A giant he was . . . he *adored* your mother, may she rest in piece, worshipped the ground she walked on . . .

Mike Tell me, Mrs Green, is that right? You have a son from my grandfather?

Mrs Green I owe it to myself and I owe it to him who was the father of my child, and to the blood of his children . . . He loved your mother and nothing can take that away. You were his life and nothing else mattered . . . nothing, not me, anything . . . Yet he grew fond of me . . . and needed to talk . . . to unburden himself . . .

Debby He had my darling mother to talk to . . . She listened . . . He had us . . . *We* listened!

Mrs Green Of course he did, but he felt you didn't understand what he needed . . .

Debby 'Ooh, my wife doesn't understand me!' Sure!

Mike It doesn't help, Ma, if we are impatient with Mrs Green . . . or aggressive . . . The lady has come of her own accord to pay respects . . .

Sam Mike, quite right. You must hear the lady out . . . Anger in the house . . . is like a worm in a plant . . .

Morris All right, let her have her say.

Betty A mouth is a door . . . and should be kept closed!

Mike Look, while we may not like what she says, while it may upset you, Ma, or shock us, the truth will always come out . . .

Sam He's right! Truth hurts, but it's clean and the wound will heal . . .

Mrs Green Thank you, Mr . . .

Sam Hyman . . . I'm the second son and so *your* son is my half-brother! Shirly, get Mrs Green some tea . . .

Shirly I don't think so . . . I think it's better that she goes. This is *our* ceremony, our 'sit and shiver' . . . So write a letter, Mrs Green . . . Tell us everything in a letter . . .

Mike Shirl, leave her be . . . She has a son, she claims, from Grandad, so if that is true he's a kind of an uncle to you! And to me!

Shirly Oh, no no no!

Mike What's so terrible? What's such a crime that someone fell in love after twenty years of marriage . . .? So this is the day of truth . . . Today we come to speak of Monte Hyman and to revere his memory . . .

Mrs Green That's why I came . . . I felt I *had* to. I was alone, all alone . . . Nobody to share it with, no one I could grieve with . . .

Betty 'You may regret your silence once but you will regret your talk twice!'

Lionel Betty, now she's here, let her speak! What about your son? Where is *he*?

Mrs Green Louis left home years ago . . . There was nothing to hold him here . . . I seldom hear from him . . .

Mike Why? Didn't you have a loving relationship? Didn't he care for you?

Mrs Green I think he hated me, even though he loved me at the same time . . . He felt left out and seldom could see his father . . . So he was the son of a father and yet not a son, he was an orphan and not . . . So he knew there was another life, where his father ate with his children and talked to them, but this was not for him . . .

Debby I can't believe this.

Lionel Shh, shh, shh.

Mrs Green It's true, for our son, only isolation, embarrassment at school . . . 'What does your father do?' In the end it was easier to say that he was dead . . . In the early days Monte would come and spend a weekend –

Debby Oy, oy!

Mrs Green – but it was hard, so hard because he was afraid . . .

Debby So he *should* be!

Mrs Green With us he had a half-life in the shadows.

Mike Did he look after you?

Mrs Green Oh yes. He wouldn't let us starve . . . of course not. But he lived in fear of being found out . . . It haunted him . . .

Debby Ohh!

Shirly You must go! Mother doesn't want to hear any more . . . What are you trying to do to us?

Betty I agree . . . The less you talk, the healthier!

Mrs Green I only wanted to tell you my story . . .

Lionel So let her finish . . . It's best it's all out . . .

Mrs Green You see, he loved you, but he also loved me and our son.

Debby *Oy*, a *broch!* We don't need to hear this!

Mrs Green But he would never have left you . . . never!

Debby Because he was a *mensch* . . . He loved my mother and he worshipped the ground she walked on . . . You were an aberration!

Mrs Green Of course he loved you, he was a supporter, a breadwinner, but he felt that he wasn't . . .

Morris What *wasn't* he, Mrs Green? What are you trying to tell us? You know you are hurting the family . . .

Debby 'You can't protect yourself against a thief in your own house!'

Sam 'All theft depends on a receiver!'

Shirly You see what you're doing, Mrs Green? Is that why you came here . . . to give us pain?

Mrs Green No, never . . . That's not it . . . He felt that I respected him, gave him love and respect . . .

Morris Are you saying that his children and wife – God rest her soul – *didn't*? Is *that* what you're saying?

Betty Everybody respected him . . . He was loved and respected by everybody . . .

Debby Why do you answer her? The woman's mad!

Sylv I think she's sad, and I think it would be kindest to hear her out . . .

Debby Another one who wants to wreck the family!

Mike No one wants to wreck anything! The woman's grief is for Grandad and she wanted to share it with you and we should be whole enough, sane enough, to accept it . . . We are not perfect . . . Mrs Green, thank you for coming and telling us this story, your story of Grandad. Now we will try to come to grips with it . . . Sam's right, it's healthier to have the truth . . .

Mrs Green Thank you . . . I just wanted to say . . . that you have another part of your family and that your blood flows in another's veins.

Mike I'm glad you told us.

Mrs Green We kept away for twenty-five years, so as not to hurt you or cause you shame . . . But at death the truth must be told . . . At death there should be no secrets, and I am not asking for anything . . . If we are afraid to speak the truth, then what are we? Less than human . . . Living for what we choose to believe . . . With love there can be no sin, Mrs Levin. Your father was a good man . . . God bless you . . .

Mrs Green exits. There is a moment of silence before Betty speaks.

Betty 'For a long happy life, breathe through your nose and keep your mouth shut!'

SCENE THREE

Sam 'It's not the mouse but the hole that's the thief . . .'

Debby A curse on her . . . A curse on her guts . . . May you rot in hell, you *farshtinkener shiksa* . . . Shirly, why did you let her in . . .? Why . . .?

Shirly How was I to know? She came to the door and said she was a friend . . .

Mike Maybe it's good . . . Yes! Maybe it's good to let a little air into the house . . .

Shirly I can't believe it . . .

Betty Who knows if she's telling the truth? I mean, why do you take her word?

Debby Betty, thank God . . . A bit of sense . . .

Betty I mean, a crazy woman comes in with a cock-and-bull story, and you all believe her?

Morris Betty's right . . . You have to check the story, get addresses, birth certificates . . .

Sam (*dominating*) Let's take it easy for a moment. Okay, Shirly, be a darling and make some more tea . . .

Betty You'll pish like a race horse!

Morris I'm very curious why should she do such a thing.

Mike I wonder what this son of hers looks like?

Debby *There's no son!!*

Mike Ma . . . Ma. Just *if* . . . I mean, it's possible . . . She *did* work for him all those years ago . . . Maybe something happened . . . It's just possible . . .

Debby Then she tricked him! That's what they do . . . They get themselves pregnant to hook them for life . . . A one-night stand . . . maybe . . . If such a thing would be possible . . . And in his heart he didn't want to let her down . . .

Shirly Ma! Not all the world is evil and we're the only ones in the right . . . Everyone else is no good . . . plotting against us . . . The sun doesn't always shine out of our arses . . .

Debby No! No! No! Not those vulgar words today!

Shirly (*to everyone*) Well it *doesn't* . . . There's a poor woman out there . . . in the cold, neglected, alienated . . .

Made to feel like a leper because of guilt . . . Not wishing to disturb our vision of the wholesome Yiddisher family, the noble patriarch . . . And so if it's true – and we must be prepared to face that possibility – then they suffered, were left out, made to feel wretched . . . So we should not feel tainted . . . to keep up the sham . . . It's hypocritical. You can't *always* be right . . .

Debby What are you talking about, Shirly? A *shiksa* working part-time took advantage of a vulnerable man . . . of his weakness . . .

Shirly No, no, not a *shiksa*, a human being, a vulnerable ordinary, decent human being –

Debby Ahhck!

Shirly – who maybe, who knows, gave Grandad a bit of happiness . . . Let's rid ourselves of those ugly words, the labels that make us feel superior . . . The chosen ones . . . Maybe . . . and this is what you might have to face . . . maybe our *own* lives were made better 'cause Grandad was happier . . . So you . . . we . . . were the receivers of that happiness while *she* stayed in the shadows . . .

Sam Good girl, Shirly . . .

Shirly It's terrible, terrible . . . And now I feel shame for the way I too wanted to get rid of her as if she was some kind of worthless thing . . . I want to see the poor woman who had the guts to come here and open her heart to us . . . to reconcile . . . take her to us . . .

Sam Shirly, you make a good case . . . You should be a lawyer . . . If things aren't the way you like, like them the way they are . . . Now make us a fresh pot of tea, there's a good girl!

Betty Can't you *ever* stop drinking tea? I don't know where you put it . . .

Debby This is the way my own flesh and blood speaks to her mother . . .

Shirly Who else wants tea . . . Mike, Sylv?

Mike Yes please, both with milk . . .

Debby I can't believe there'd arrive the day when my own flesh and blood berates me in public . . .

Lionel Debby! Enough already.

Debby (*taken aback*) What? Enough. Do you care, do you? A beast enters our home, spreads havoc and all you can say is *enough* – like you can never be bothered – you never could be *bothered*, take a *stand*. That's you, just sit back. 'Enough.'

Lionel (*warning*) Debby.

Morris Stop it, Lionel, she's upset.

Lionel From you, from you – I've had enough – from that mouth bigger than the Blackwall Tunnel I've had enough from your constant moaning, self-pitying . . . I've had enough – yes – that's right.

Morris Lionel.

Lionel No, she's right. I've sat back, said nothing to her years of whingeing, years! . . . Like she's the only one who feels, she's the only one with pain, a big blob, crying 'Me! Me! Me!' And I put up with it. Yes, Morris, I put up with it to retain peace, sanity in the house, and for the kids – but now – yes! Now I say to you – Debby, I have had enough – okay, enough! Enough!

 Silence.

Debby Did you hear that? Did you hear how he speaks to me?

Betty Even a flea can bite!

Mike Shh now – hey, come on. Look, if what Mrs Green says is true, then isn't it better to be friends than enemies? I mean, what's the point of that? It's a waste of life and you learn nothing about each other . . . We may find that this young man's a great guy and that he brings something to us . . . eh, Uncle Sam?

Sam I bet if he became an Albert Einstein you wouldn't disclaim him . . . If in a few years time he became a multi-millionaire and wanted to meet his relatives, I'd like to see you throw him out!

Morris My God, he's right!

Debby They're all against me . . . I can't believe it . . .

Lionel We're not against you.

Sam No one's against you . . . Just relax and have a cuppa . . .

Shirly Ma, you want some tea?

Debby Who can drink tea now? My throat is like dry leather . . .

Shirly So have some tea . . .

Debby Tea won't help it, Shirly . . . Not tea . . . *Acid* you force me to drink . . . I drink the acid of your wicked tongue . . .!

Shirly (*sharp*) Then wash it down with tea . . .

Debby She thinks it funny! I swear, she thinks it funny!

Mike (*celebrating*) Now I've got a half-brother . . . or a half-uncle, I suppose . . .

Debby You want to rub the shame in my face?!

Sam I have such memories of Mother – God rest her soul – what a woman . . . But to tell the truth and forgive me, Dad, she had a lot to put up with . . . and that's the truth . . . So many times I'd visit and see her sitting alone . . . Alone and neglected because he was with someone else . . .

Debby Sam, don't . . . Not on a day like this . . .

Sam Maybe, Debby . . . Yes . . . on a day like this! It's okay . . . Maybe that was his nature and he couldn't help it . . . Maybe that's all he knew . . . But believe me, he was no saint . . . He persecuted you and if you dared to complain it was a clump . . . But the worst, the very worst, was the neglect of your mother . . . and the poor woman accepted it . . . So maybe it's good that Mrs Green came . . . Maybe she opened the cupboard and the stink comes out . . . That my father was a bastard . . . So what are we covering it up for, eh? He hastened your mother's end . . . the nights he spent away . . . in the Turkish baths . . . He'd claim, 'Don't nag! I was playing cards . . . Leave me alone . . .' Just because he brought home a big bag of fruit or some deli . . . Guilt offerings, Debby! He thought he was a *mensch* . . . He couldn't help it . . . There she lay . . . I can never forget . . . Alone, bored, neglected . . . Her sickness eating into her like rust . . . *That's* what I remember: the pain, the sorrow . . . I watched her slowly go . . . Debby, lets face it. Why do you deny it?

Mike So what happened? What happened to Grandma?

Debby She kept *shtum* . . . to protect the kids . . . Because she knew he'd explode . . .

Mike How could she stay with him? . . . How could she put up with it . . . ?

Lionel 'Better pain in your heart than shame on your face . . .'

Morris (*to Mike*) Son, it's a slow process . . . It starts with a few small liberties backed up by a bit of a threat . . . You accept less, your threshold gets lower, you accept less for what you think is a bit of peace . . . Slowly your life erodes . . . You don't complain or, if you do, the result isn't worth it . . . until in the end you have been conditioned to accept anything . . . for some peace of mind . . . for the kids . . . You trade your beliefs of a dream for a terrible compromise . . . for appearances . . . You hide your shame . . .

Mike So in a way you're ashamed of your own shame . . .

Sam Is Sylv still with us? She's been so quiet, I thought she'd gone . . .

Sylv Well, I don't like to say too much . . . I mean, it's all very personal to you . . .

Shirly leaves the room.

Sam So, Sylv, what do you think we should do?

Sylv Oh, I don't know . . . It's so difficult . . . I think it's healthy, though, when secrets are exposed . . . I mean, human nature is what it is . . . You can't legislate against human nature, I think . . . You try . . . you make laws – moral laws – but what are they? . . . Just guides, I suppose. Nature will come out and assert itself – I expect it *has* to. Nature's more powerful than us . . . We can't make laws against nature to protect ourselves, can we, Mike?

Sam (*with spirit*) Very good . . . That's *exactly* what I was saying earlier . . . How many of us wouldn't be here if we all obeyed the coventional laws? . . . We'd be a few geniuses short . . .

Mike Ahh . . . So you protected Grandad 'cause you were ashamed . . .

Lionel (*about Monte*) A wasted life, if you ask me . . .

Debby 'Evil came into the house like a worm in a fruit . . .'

Shirly comes in with a tea tray.

Shirly Tea's up!

They all dive in. Ad-lib: noisy, with an element of relief, a purging.

Mike Mine's with sugar . . .

Sylv No sugar for me . . . I'm so thirsty.

Sam Two sugars . . . Which is mine?

Shirly With the spoon is two sugars. No spoon is no sugars.

Mike The blue cup is one sugar. Eat some fishcakes.

Shirly Ma, you wanna cup?

Debby Yeah, but a milky one!

Shirly This is milky – take this one . . .

Debby But that one's got the sugar in it . . .

Lionel Does it matter? So I'll drink it . . .

Mike Ma, don't worry about it any more . . .

Debby A horse has a huge head, so let *him* worry!

Sam You know, the last of the Yiddish theatres has closed in New York?

Betty Oy! He's back in New York again!

Sam Some of the greatest actors performed there. Luther Adler, Paul Muny, Morris Karnofsky. Do you know, I once saw *King Lear* in Yiddish?

Mike That must have been really something, Sam.

Sam Well, *Lear* is like a Yiddish play. Here's a father who thinks he's hard done by because a daughter speaks the truth. Tells him she loves him with qualifications. Oh, he can't take that, oh no.

Morris Nobody likes hearing their faults exposed. So you lie to keep the peace. I told you. Who wants truth these days? We're a nation of smilers and liars. Have a nice day!

Betty (*laugh*) So what happened to the old man? I could never understand Shakespeare. I don't know what the fuss is about.

Debby So Sam, oh he's so clever, what happened?

Sam Well, everybody supported the old man, Lear, in his obsession until he went mad. He cracked up.

'Howl, howl, howl, howl.'

Sam gets up and performs Lear like a man possessed.

'Blow winds and crack your cheeks! Rage, blow.
You cataracts and hurricanoes spout
Till you have drenched our steeples.'

All clap.

Morris Hey, you're a born actor, Sam.

Betty He should have been. He knows his Shakespeare.

Sam The only play I could do now is Oedipus.

Debby Oedipus, who's Oedipus?

Sam Yes, Oedipus. He killed his father and slept with his mother. And when he realised what he's done he tears his eyes out.

Debby Ooh, that's disgusting. Now Sam, please no more. This is our father's sit and shiver.

Lionel No one's eating the fishcakes!

Freeze. Music. Everyone dances off. Blackout.

Glossary of Yiddish Words and Phrases

Alter schmutters old rags

Bissle little

Blintz pancake

Broch calamity

Bubeleh term of endearment to a grandmother / child

Dollalla little doll

Dreck crap

Farshtinkener stinking

Frummers religious

Ganeff thief

Gei gehsunt go in good health

Gelt money

Gevalt goodness

Gott in Himmel God in Heaven

Goyim non-Jew

Kibitzing talking

Kishkas guts

Kopf head

Kvetch complain

Mensch good person

Mishuga mad

Mitzvah commandment / good work

Momzer bastard

Mumella little mother

Oy vay oh dear

Schlep drag

Schmaltz cooking fat / corny

Schmooze get round someone

Schmuck fool

Shaynalla dearest

Shiksa non-Jewish woman

Shivah seven / period of mourning

Shlemiel fool

Shtetl small town

Schtipping fornicating

Shtum silent

Spieler gambler

Tuchis bottom

Tucker indeed